STEEL DESIGN

daab

Introduction 4

The buildings that make up the urban structure of every city in the world do not just function as housing apartments, public centers and offices, some have clearly been designed to be works of art.

To this end, architecture has advanced quickly and effectively, principally in the field of constructive materials, which are fundamental when fulfilling the dream of raising one of these massive structures. Amongst the materials that have had most influence in the creation of this new architecture is steel; the result of a carbon-iron alloy, which is impressively ductile, resistant and tough.

The architectural precedent of these large buildings, where steel plays a major role, is the Home Insurance building in Chicago, built in 1885 by architect William Le Baron Jenney. To support this ten-story construction, considered to be the world's first skyscraper, Jenney designed a steel framework that would hold all the floors and external walls. From then onwards, steel became one of the most fundamental materials for the 20th century's industrial society.

Today, steel is not just present in the structures and claddings of all types of buildings, it is also used in designs for household objects and plays a major role in avant-garde interior design. Due to its long life, its capacity to neutralize the effects of climatic factors and its amazing power to adapt to any shape, contemporary architects and designers have given steel a distinguishing significance in modern times.

Die großen Gebäude, die die Struktur aller Städte der Welt bilden, nehmen heutzutage nicht nur Wohnungen, öffentliche Zentren und Büroräume auf, sondern einige von ihnen wurden mit der klaren Absicht geplant, ein Kunstwerk zu schaffen.

Um dieses Ziel zu erreichen, hat die Architektur schnelle und effiziente Fortschritte gemacht, vor allem im Bereich der Konstruktionsmaterialien, die grundlegend dafür sind, die Ideen und Träume der Planer umzusetzen und große Strukturen zu errichten. Eines der Materialien, das einen starken Einfluss auf das Entstehen dieses neuen Architekturstils hatte und hat, ist der Stahl, eine Eisen-Kohlenstoff-Legierung, die sich durch ihre Verformbarkeit, Haltbarkeit und Härte auszeichnet.

Der architektonische Vorläufer der großen Gebäude, in denen Stahl eine Hauptrolle spielt, ist das Gebäude Home Insurance in Chicago, das 1885 von dem Architekten William Le Baron Jenney gebaut wurde. Um dieses zehnstöckige Gebäude zu errichten, das als der erste Wolkenkratzer der Welt betrachtet wird, konstruierte Jenney ein Stahlgerüst, das die Stockwerke und die Außenwände des Gebäudes trägt. Das war der Zeitpunkt, zu dem Stahl zu einem der Hauptmaterialien der Industriegesellschaft des 20. Jh. wurde.

Heutzutage findet man Stahl nicht nur in den Strukturen und Verkleidungen aller möglichen Gebäudetypen, sondern er wird auch zum Gestalten von Haushaltsobjekten des täglichen Gebrauchs benutzt, und er spielt eine Hauptrolle bei der Innengestaltung avantgardistischster Wohnumgebungen. Aufgrund seiner Haltbarkeit, seiner Wetterbeständigkeit und seiner enormen Anpassungsfähigkeit an jegliche Form entscheiden sich immer mehr Architekten und Innenarchitekten für dieses Material. Somit ist Stahl zu einem Kennzeichen der heutigen Zeit geworden.

Los edificios que conforman la estructura urbanística de las ciudades de todo el mundo no sólo tienen la función de albergar viviendas, centros públicos y oficinas, sino que algunos de ellos han sido ideados con la clara intención de convertirse en obras de arte.

Para poder conseguir este objetivo, la arquitectura ha avanzado de forma rápida y eficaz, principalmente en el campo de los materiales constructivos, los cuales resultan fundamentales a la hora de materializar el sueño de levantar grandes estructuras. Entre los materiales que más han influido en la creación de esta nueva arquitectura se encuentra el acero, metal procedente de una aleación entre el hierro y el carbono, que destaca por su ductilidad, resistencia y dureza.

El Home Insurance de Chicago, construido en 1885 por el arquitecto William Le Baron Jenney, es el precedente arquitectónico de los grandes edificios en los que el acero tiene un protagonismo principal. Para conseguir esta construcción de diez plantas, considerada el primer rascacielos del mundo, Jenney ideó un armazón de acero, a fin de que soportase los diversos pisos y las paredes externas del edificio. A partir de ese momento, el acero se convirtió en uno de los materiales fundamentales para la sociedad industrial del siglo XX.

En la actualidad, el acero no sólo está presente en las estructuras y recubrimientos de todo tipo de edificios, sino que también se utiliza en el diseño de objetos de uso doméstico y es protagonista del interiorismo de las casas más vanguardistas. Por su larga duración, su capacidad de neutralizar los efectos de los factores climáticos y el enorme poder de adaptación a cualquier forma, los arquitectos y diseñadores contemporáneos se han rendido al acero para convertirlo en una seña de identidad de los tiempos que corren.

Les édifices qui façonnent la structure du paysage urbain des villes du monde entier n'ont pas tous pour seule fonction d'accueillir des habitations, centres publics et bureaux. En effet, certains sont clairement conçus pour devenir des œuvres d'art.

Pour y parvenir, l'architecture a évolué d'une manière rapide et efficace, surtout dans le domaine des matériaux de construction, éléments clés à l'heure de réaliser le rêve d'édification de grandes structures. Parmi ceux qui ont fortement influencé la création de cette nouvelle architecture, citons l'acier, métal issu d'un alliage entre le fer et le carbone, réputé pour sa ductilité, résistance et robustesse.

Le Home Insurance de Chicago, construit en 1885 par l'architecte William Le Baron Jenney, est le premier exemple architectonique de grands édifices où l'acier joue le rôle principal. Pour soutenir cette construction de dix étages, considérée comme le premier gratte-ciel du monde, Jenney a conçu une armature d'acier sur laquelle reposent étages et murs extérieurs. Dés lors, l'acier est devenu l'un des matériaux phares de la société industrielle du XXe siècle.

A l'heure actuelle, l'acier n'est pas uniquement l'apanage des structures et habillages d'édifices en tout genre. Egalement présent dans le design d'objets à usage domestique, l'acier est aussi le protagoniste de l'architecture d'intérieur des maisons avant-gardistes. Grâce à sa durabilité, capacité de neutraliser les effets des incidences climatiques et malléabilité lui permettant d'épouser toutes les formes, l'acier, devenu le matériau par excellence des architectes et designers contemporains, scelle l'identité de notre époque.

Gli edifici che compongono la struttura urbanistica delle città di tutto il mondo non svolgono solo la funzione di ospitare case, centri pubblici e uffici; alcuni di essi sono stati costruiti con la chiara intenzione di creare opere d'arte.

Per raggiungere quest'obiettivo, l'architettura ha fatto rapidi ed efficaci passi avanti, principalmente nel campo dei materiali da costruzione, che risultano cruciali per poter concretizzare il sogno di dar vita a grandi strutture. Tra i materiali che più hanno contribuito alla nascita di questa nuova architettura si trova l'acciaio, un metallo ottenuto da una lega di ferro e carbonio, dotato di una particolare duttilità, resistenza e durezza.

Il precedente architettonico dei grandi edifici in cui l'acciaio ha un ruolo da protagonista va cercato nell'Home Insurance di Chicago, costruito nel 1885 dall'architetto William Le Baron Jenney. Per sostenere questa costruzione di dieci piani, considerata il primo grattacielo del mondo, Jenney ideò un'impalcatura d'acciaio capace di reggere il peso dei vari piani e delle pareti esterne. Da quel momento in poi, l'acciaio cominciò ad essere considerato uno dei materiali più importati in uso nella società industriale del XX secolo.

Oggi, l'acciaio non è presente solo all'interno delle strutture e dei rivestimenti di edifici di ogni tipo, ma è utilizzato anche nella realizzazione di oggetti domestici svolgendo un ruolo di primo piano nell'arredo degli interni più alla vanguardia. Grazie alla sua lunga durata, alla capacità di resistere agli effetti dei fattori climatici e alla sua adattabilità a soluzioni formali di ogni tipo, oggi l'acciaio è assurto al ruolo di materiale principe per architetti e designer che lo hanno così trasformato nel marchio di fabbrica della contemporaneità.

BCQ – BAENA, CASAMOR & QUERA ARQUITECTES | BARCELONA
PORT FORUM 2004
Barcelona, Spain | 2006

Despite the contemporary appearance of this group of buildings and constructions, the use of corten steel as the primary material, both in the structures and for the finishes, transports us to a more traditional dockland image. The image of shells of boats abandoned to their fate can be seen in the steel cubes that house the bars.

Obwohl diese Hafenanlage sehr modern wirkt, entsteht durch die Verwendung von Stahl als wichtigstem Material an den Strukturen und Verkleidungen doch ein fast traditionelles Bild. Die alten Rümpfe verlassener Schiffe verschmelzen mit den Stahlwürfeln, in denen sich die Gaststätten befinden.

A pesar de la contemporaneidad de este conjunto de edificios y construcciones, la utilización del acero corten como material principal, tanto para las estructuras como para los revestimientos, nos sugiere una imagen portuaria tradicional. La visión de los viejos cascos de barco abandonados a su suerte se confunden con los cubos de acero que albergan los bares.

En dépit du caractère contemporain de cet ensemble d'édifices et de constructions, l'utilisation de l'acier comme matière principale, tant pour les structures que pour les revêtements, nous transporte vers une image portuaire traditionnelle. La vision des vieilles coques de bateau abandonnées à leur sort se confond avec les cubes d'acier accueillant les bars.

Nonostante la contemporaneità di questo complesso di edifici e costruzioni, l'impiego dell'acciaio Corten come materiale principale, sia per le strutture che per i rivestimenti, rimanda ad un'immagine portuaria tradizionale. La vista dei vecchi scafi delle imbarcazioni abbandonati al loro destino si confonde con quella dei cubi di acciaio che accolgono i bar.

BERNARD TSCHUMI ARCHITECTS | NEW YORK
CONCERT HALL AND EXHIBITION COMPLEX
Rouen, France | 2001

Breaking with the tradition of auditoriums as sober places, this architects studio created a monumental, multipurpose space in which a variety of events could be organized, ranging from rock concerts to political meetings. Along with many other features this oval building stands out for its use of steel both in the structure and the exterior cladding.

Um das Klischee zu widerlegen, dass ein Konzertsaal ein nüchterner Ort ist, hat das Architekturstudio ein monumentales, multifunktionelles Gebäude geschaffen, das sich für verschiedene Arten von Veranstaltungen eignet, so zum Beispiel Rockkonzerte oder politische Veranstaltungen. Neben vielen anderen interessanten Einzelheiten fällt an diesem Gebäude auf, wie man Stahl sowohl für die Struktur als auch für die äußere Verkleidung benutzte.

Rompiendo con el tópico de un auditorio como un lugar sobrio, el estudio de arquitectos creó un monumental espacio multiusos en el que se pueden organizar diversos actos, desde conciertos de rock hasta mítines políticos. Este edificio ovalado destaca, entre muchas otras características, por la utilización del acero tanto en la estructura como en el recubrimiento exterior.

En rupture avec le cliché de l'auditorium lieu de sobriété, le cabinet d'architectes a créé un espace multiusage monumental qui peut accueillir divers événements, des concerts de rock jusqu'aux réunions politiques. Ovale, cet édifice est remarquable, entre autres caractéristiques, par l'utilisation de l'acier tant pour la structure que pour le revêtement extérieur.

Stravolgendo la tipica immagine di un auditorio visto come un luogo sobrio, questo studio di architetti ha creato un monumentale spazio multiuso in cui si possono organizzare diversi eventi, da concerti rock fino a meeting politici. Tra le varie caratteristiche, questo edificio di forma ovale si fa notare per l'impiego dell'acciaio sia nell'orditura interna che nel rivestimento esterno.

BERNARD TSCHUMI ARCHITECTS | NEW YORK
VACHERON CONSTANTIN HEADQUARTERS AND WATCH FACTORY
Geneva, Switzerland | 2004

This building that houses the factory and offices of an old watch manufacturer, was conceived as a modern, space for creation that offered continuity to a company with a long history. In an attempt to link the past with the present, a flexible building was designed with organic forms and multiple levels. Outside, the structure is finished by way of a steel mesh.

Dieses Gebäude, in dem sich eine Fabrik und die Büros eines renommierten Uhrherstellers befinden, wurde wie ein moderner Ort der schöpferischen Arbeit gestaltet, der die lange Tradition eines alten Unternehmens fortsetzt. Um die Vergangenheit mit der Gegenwart zu verbinden, wurde ein flexibles Gebäude mit organischen Formen und vielen Ebenen geschaffen. Von außen ist die Struktur mit einem Metallnetz aus Stahl verkleidet.

Este edificio, que alberga la fábrica y las oficinas de una antigua marca de relojes, fue concebido como un moderno espacio de creación que daba continuidad a una empresa de larga tradición. Con la voluntad de aunar pasado con presente, se ideó un edificio flexible, de formas orgánicas y con múltiples niveles. Exteriormente, la estructura se recubrió con una malla metálica de acero.

Cet immeuble abrite la fabrique et les bureaux d'une marque de montre historique. Il a été conçu comme un espace moderne de création qui assure la continuité d'une entreprise à la longue tradition. Dans l'idée de mesurer le passé et le présent, l'édifice a été voulu flexible, avec des formes organiques et des niveaux multiples. Extérieurement, la structure a été recouverte d'un maillage métallique en acier.

Questo edificio che ospita la fabbrica e gli uffici di un antico marchio di orologi, è stato concepito come un moderno spazio di creazione che dava continuità ad un'azienda di lunga tradizione. Con l'idea di unire il passato al presente, si è progettato un edificio flessibile, dalle forme organiche e dai molteplici livelli. Esteriormente la struttura è stata rivestita da una rete metallica di acciaio.

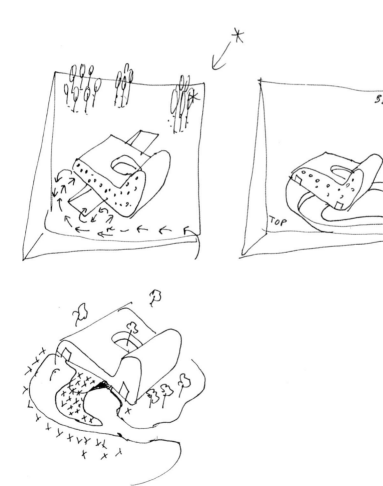

BOTTOM

TOP

Since it was built, for the Expo 58, the iconic image of the Atomium has stood up to the test of time. Its appearance, however, has not. With the aim of recovering the past shine of this 390-foot high molecule, it was subjected to a thorough restoration. The original aluminum of the spheres was replaced by a stainless steel skin on the outside, and a galvanized steel skin on the inside. A new town square, which looks onto this statuesque structure, and a steel clad pavilion housing the ticket office and toilets have been added to the construction, bringing it back to modern times.

Das für die Weltausstellung 1958 errichtete Atomium in Brüssel hat dem Lauf der Zeit widerstanden und wurde zur Ikone und dem Kennzeichen der Stadt. Allerdings hat seine Oberfläche in dieser Zeit etwas gelitten. Damit das 102 Meter hohe Molekül wieder in seinem alten Glanz erstrahlt, wurden umfassende Renovierungsmaßnahmen durchgeführt. So ersetzte man das originale Aluminium der Kugeln außen durch eine Haut aus Edelstahl und innen durch galvanisierten Stahl. Dem Atomium wurde außerdem ein neuer städtischer Platz hinzugefügt, von dem aus man es betrachten kann, und ein mit Stahl verkleideter Pavillon, in dem die Eintrittskarten verkauft werden und die Infrastruktur untergebracht ist, so dass die gesamte Baugruppe wieder modern und avantgardistisch wirkt.

Desde que se construyó para la Expo 58, la icónica imagen del Atomium ha resistido el paso del tiempo. No así su apariencia. Con el objetivo de que la molécula de 102 metros de altura recupere su brillo de antaño, se realizó una profunda remodelación. Así el aluminio original de las esferas fue sustituido por una piel de acero, inoxidable en el exterior y galvanizado en el interior. Una nueva plaza urbana desde la que admirar la estructura escultural y un pabellón revestido de acero, que aloja la oficina de venta de billetes y los servicios, han sido agregados al conjunto, que vuelve a respirar modernidad.

Depuis sa construction, pour l'Expo 58, l'image iconique de l'Atomium a résisté au passage du temps, contrairement à son apparence extérieure. Pour que la molécule de 102 mètres de haut retrouve l'éclat d'antan, elle a été complètement remodelée. L'aluminium original des sphères est remplacé par une enveloppe extérieure en acier inoxydable, galvanisée à l'intérieur. Une nouvelle place urbaine, d'où le passant peut admirer la structure sculpturale et un pavillon revêtu d'acier, accueillant l'espace de vente des tickets et des services, se sont ajoutés à l'ensemble, qui respire ainsi à nouveau la modernité.

Da quando l'Atomium fu costruito per l'Expo 58, la sua immagine d'icona non è stata intaccata dal trascorrere del tempo. Lo stesso non può dirsi del suo aspetto. Per far sì che la molecola di 102 metri d'altezza recuperasse lo splendore di un tempo, sono stati realizzati importanti lavori di ristrutturazione. A questo scopo l'alluminio della sfera originale è stato sostituito da una pelle d'acciaio inox nella parte esterna, e galvanizzato all'interno. La ristrutturazione è stata completata dalla costruzione di una nuova piazza urbana, da cui ammirare la struttura scultoria, e da un padiglione rivestito in acciaio che ospita biglietteria e servizi. In questo modo ora il complesso può fare sfoggio di una nuova aria di modernità.

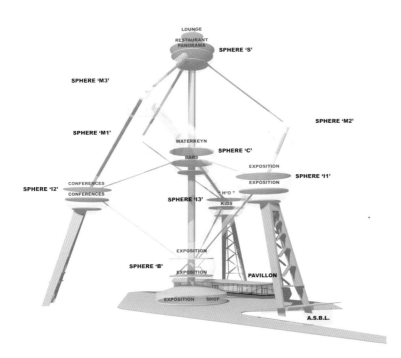

LOUNGE
RESTAURANT
PANORAMA   SPHERE 'S'

SPHERE 'M3'

                                        SPHERE 'M2'

SPHERE 'M1'

            WATERKEYN
              BARS   SPHERE 'C'

                                    EXPOSITION
                        CONFERENCES   EXPOSITION   SPHERE 'I1'
SPHERE 'I2'   CONFERENCES
                                    SPHERE 'I3'   " H²O "
                                                      KIDS

                            EXPOSITION

SPHERE 'B'   EXPOSITION   PAVILLON

                    EXPOSITION   SHOP

                                                A.S.B.L.

This house was designed between dividing walls in an outlying neighborhood, which is not recognized for its quality of town planning and architecture. The house has large windows on both the front and back façades. These openings, which once illuminated by fluorescent lights give the building the appearance of an ice cube, are possible due to the highly resistant steel structure.

In diesem Stadtrandviertel, das sich weder durch eine gelungene städtebauliche Planung noch durch schöne Architektur auszeichnet, plante man dieses Reihenhaus, ein Einfamilienhaus mit großen Fenstern an der Vorder-und Hinterfassade. Wenn diese Fenster mit Leuchtstoffröhren beleuchtet sind, nimmt das Gebäude das Aussehen eines Eiswürfels an. Eine Stahlstruktur machte das Öffnen der großen Fensterflächen möglich.

Esta casa entre medianeras fue construida en un barrio periférico que no destaca por su nivel urbanístico ni arquitectónico. Se trata de una vivienda unifamiliar con grandes ventanales tanto en la fachada delantera como en la posterior. Estas aberturas, que una vez iluminadas por fluorescentes dan al edificio el aspecto de un cubito de hielo, tienen su origen en la resistente estructura de acero.

Cette maison mitoyenne a été créée entre dans un quartier de la périphérie qui ne se distingue aucunement par son urbanisme ou son architecture. Une maison familiale aux grandes baies vitrées, tant sur la façade avant que sur l'arrière. Ces ouvertures, qui une fois éclairées par des lumières fluorescentes donnent à la construction l'aspect d'un glaçon, trouvent leur origine dans la structure résistante en acier.

In un quartiere periferico che non spicca certo per il livello urbanistico né per quello architettonico, è stata disegnata questa casa tra vari muri di mezzeria. Un'abitazione unifamiliare che presenta grandi vetrate sia nella facciata anteriore che posteriore. Queste aperture sorrette da un'intelaiatura di acciaio, una volta illuminate dai neon, danno all'edificio le sembianze di un cubetto di ghiaccio.

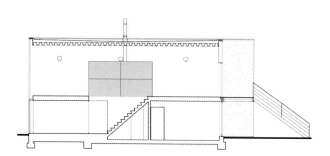

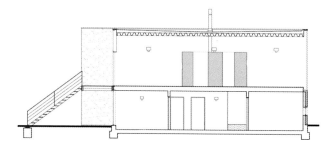

50

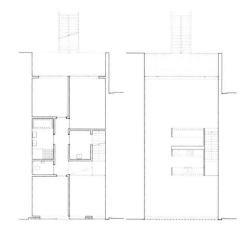

The image of this building is that of an immense transparent box, which is raised from the ground. The design of this house, a low-budget project, stands out for the use of steel as its primary constructive material. This material is found both in the building's structure, which allows for an open-plan and the entry of a large amount of light, and in the finish of the exterior walls.

Dieses Gebäude wirkt wie eine riesige, transparente Kiste, die sich vom Boden abhebt. Das Haus, für dessen Errichtung nur ein kleines Budget zur Verfügung stand, fällt vor allem durch die Verwendung von Stahl als wichtigstem Konstruktionsmaterial auf. Und zwar wurde sowohl für die Struktur des Gebäudes als auch für die Verkleidung der Außenwände Stahl verwendet, so dass ein durchgehendes, transparent wirkendes, helles Stockwerk entstand.

Al observar este edificio se tiene la impresión de estar ante una inmensa caja transparente levantada del suelo. El diseño de esta casa, un proyecto de bajo presupuesto, destaca por la utilización del acero como principal material constructivo. Encontramos este material tanto en la estructura del edificio, que permite una planta diáfana y muy luminosa, como en el cubrimiento de las paredes exteriores.

La vision de cet édifice le révèle comme une immense caisse transparente s'élevant du sol. Le design de cette maison, un projet à budget réduit, se distingue par l'utilisation de l'acier comme matériau de construction principal. Ce matériau est présent tant dans la structure de l'édifice, assurant un étage diaphane et très lumineux, que dans le revêtement des parois extérieures.

Osservando questo edificio, si ha l'impressione di vedere un'immensa scatola trasparente sollevata dal terreno. Il progetto di questa casa, eseguito con un preventivo ridotto, spicca per l'impiego dell'acciaio come principale materiale costruttivo. Questo materiale è stato adoperato sia per la struttura dell'edificio che dà vita a un piano diafano e molto luminoso sia per il rivestimento delle pareti esterne.

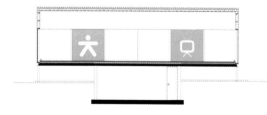

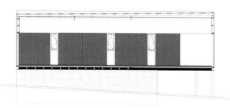

CREPAIN BINST ARCHITECTURE | ANTWERP
OFFICES FOR RENSON
Waregem, Belgium | 2002

When carrying out this project the industrial sector of the company responsible for the commission had a considerable influence. A modern, linear office building was designed, whose construction used the most advanced materials and technologies. A structure of sturdy steel columns generates this large, open-plan single story.

Bei der Planung dieses Gebäudes berücksichtigte man, dass es sich inmitten eines Industriegebietes befindet, in dem das Unternehmen tätig ist, das den Auftrag erteilte. So entwarf man ein modernes und lineares Bürogebäude, für dessen Konstruktion die fortschrittlichsten Materialien und Technologien eingesetzt wurden. Die Struktur besteht aus Stahlsäulen und formt ein einziges, geräumiges und durchgehendes Stockwerk.

Para la realización de este proyecto se tuvo muy en cuenta el sector industrial en el que trabajaba la empresa que realizó el encargo. Se diseñó un moderno y lineal edificio de oficinas, en cuya construcción se utilizaron los materiales y las tecnologías más avanzadas. Una estructura de consistentes columnas de acero da lugar a un único piso amplio y diáfano.

La réalisation de ce projet a vu principalement la prise en compte du secteur industriel auquel appartient la société commanditaire. Voit le jour un immeuble de bureaux moderne et linéaire pour la construction duquel les matériaux et techniques les plus sophistiqués ont été employés. Une structure de colonnes d'acier cohérentes crée un étage unique ample et diaphane.

Per la realizzazione di questo progetto si è tenuto particolarmente conto del settore industriale in cui operava l'azienda che ha commissionato l'incarico. Si è disegnato un edificio per uffici moderno e lineare, utilizzando per la sua costruzione i materiali e le tecnologie più avanzate. Una struttura formata da solide colonne di acciaio dà luogo a un unico piano spazioso e diafano.

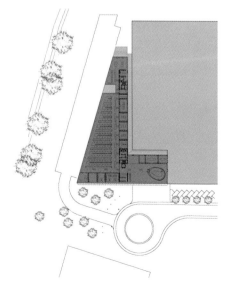

This great single-story block, with its elongated design and simple lines is the project chosen for the new headquarters of a transport company. Steel is the most commonly used material here, both in the internal and external structure of the building. The large glass windows, which allow light to enter the offices, are protected by bars of galvanized steel.

Dieser große, einstöckige Block, länglich und mit einfachen Linien, ist der neue Sitz eines Transportunternehmens. Das meistverwendete Material an diesem Gebäude ist Stahl, sowohl an der inneren als auch an der äußeren Struktur. Durch große Fenster fällt viel Licht in die Büros, und sie sind mit Gittern aus verzinktem Stahl geschützt.

Este gran bloque de sólo una planta, de diseño alargado y líneas simples, es el proyecto elegido para la nueva sede de una empresa de transportes. El acero es el material que más presencia tiene, tanto en la estructura interna del edificio como en la externa. Las grandes cristaleras, que permiten la entrada de luz a las oficinas, están protegidas por rejas de acero galvanizado.

Ce grand bloc doté d'un étage unique, au design allongé et aux lignes simples, est le projet retenu pour le nouveau siège d'une entreprise de transport. L'acier est le matériau revêtant la présence primordiale, au sein de la structure interne comme externe de l'édifice. Les grandes verrières qui facilitent l'entrée de la lumière dans les bureaux sont protégées par des grilles d'acier galvanisé.

Questo grande edificio di solo un piano, dal disegno allungato e dalle linee pure, è il progetto scelto per la nuova sede di un'impresa di trasporti. L'acciaio è il materiale che la fa da padrone, sia nella struttura interna dell'edificio che in quella esterna. Le grandi finestre che consentono di illuminare gli uffici, sono protette da ringhiere di acciaio galvanizzato.

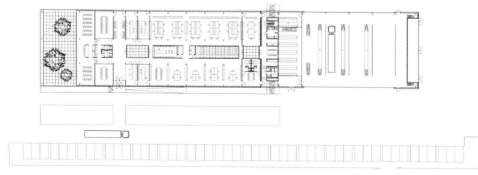

DAVID JAY WEINER | NEW YORK
ZEN GARDEN HOUSE
Crestone, United States | 2006

This interesting construction appears as a mirage in the middle of the desert and was made using a steel structure that combines rectangular forms and sharp angles. The dryness of the place did nothing to discourage the client from creating his house here, who considers the exterior to be an immense Zen garden.

Mitten in der Wüste sieht man diese interessante Konstruktion. Handelt es sich vielleicht um eine Fata Morgana? Nein, es ist eine Stahlstruktur mit rechteckigen Formen und markiert rechen Winkeln. Die Kunden ließen sich von der Dürre und Kargheit der Umgebung nicht abschrecken und bauten hier ihr Haus. Die äußere Landschaft empfinden sie wie einen riesigen Zengarten.

Esta interesante construcción aparece como un espejismo en medio del desierto. Ha sido realizada mediante una estructura de acero en la que se combinan formas rectangulares y marcados ángulos rectos. La aridez del lugar no impidió que el cliente eligiera este espacio –paisaje que él considera un inmenso jardín zen– para construir su casa.

Au milieu du désert, apparaissant comme un mirage, cette intéressante construction est réalisée grâce à une structure d'acier qui voit se combiner des formes rectangulaires et des angles droits très prononcés. L'aridité du lieu n'a aucunement constitué un obstacle au choix de cet espace par le client afin d'établir sa demeure. Il considère le paysage extérieur comme un immense jardin zen.

In mezzo al deserto appare come un miraggio questa interessante costruzione realizzata mediante una struttura di acciaio in cui si combinano forme rettangolari e accentuati angoli retti. L'aridità del posto non ha affatto costituito un ostacolo nella scelta del cliente di costruirvi la propria dimora; anzi, il paesaggio esterno viene visto da questi come un immenso giardino Zen.

DELUGAN MEISSL ASSOCIATED ARCHITECTS | VIENNA
HOUSE RAY 1
Vienna, Austria | 2003

This apartment, which boasts some magnificent terraces, was built on the roof of an office building from the seventies. To create the apartment, designed as a loft divided using varying floor levels, a large steel structure had to be designed giving greater freedom for creating the original design of the space.

Diese Wohnung hat wundervolle Terrassen und wurde auf dem Dach eines Gebäudes aus den Sechzigerjahren konstruiert. Für dieses Loft mit verschiedenen Ebenen schuf man eine große Stahlstruktur, die den Planern mehr Gestaltungsfreiheit gab.

El apartamento, que goza de unas magníficas terrazas, fue construido en la azotea de un edificio de oficinas levantado en los años sesenta. Para poder crear la vivienda, diseñada a modo de un loft dividido mediante diversos niveles de suelo, se tuvo que idear una gran estructura de acero que permitiera una mayor libertad a la hora de llevar a cabo el original diseño del piso.

L'appartement, qui jouit de magnifiques terrasses, a été construit sur le toit d'un immeuble de bureaux des années soixante. Afin de pouvoir matérialiser la demeure, pensée comme un loft divisé par divers niveaux, la conception d'une grande structure en acier s'est révélée nécessaire, pour assurer une plus grande liberté de création du design originel du logement.

L'appartamento, che comprende delle magnifiche zone esterne, è stato costruito sulla terrazza di un edificio eretto negli anni sessanta. Per poter realizzare l'originale disegno dell'appartamento, è stata creata una grande struttura in acciaio che permette di distribuire il loft su vari livelli.

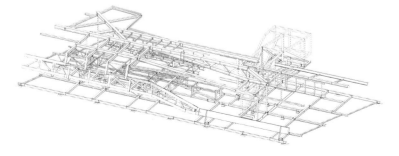

Located in the city center, the home of the Los Angeles Philharmonic Orchestra has been designed to be one of world's most acoustically sophisticated concert halls. The curved, sharp surfaces of polished stainless steel constitute a dancing mass of volumes that sparkle under the sun between the skyscrapers. The exterior's metallic cladding forms a contrast with the warmth of the wood that dominates the rows of seats and the ceiling inside the auditorium.

Mitten in der Stadt Los Angeles hat das Philharmonieorchester einen Konzertsaal errichtet, dessen Akustik weltweit eine der besten ist. Die gekrümmten und spitzen Flächen aus poliertem Edelstahl bilden eine tanzende Masse aus Formen, die zwischen den Wolkenkratzern in der Sonne glänzen. Die Metallverkleidung am Gebäudeäußeren schafft einen Kontrast zu dem warmen Holz, das in den Sitzreihen und am Dach des Auditoriums vorherrscht.

Situado en el centro de la ciudad, el hogar de la Orquesta Filarmónica de Los Ángeles ha sido diseñado como una de las salas de concierto más sofisticadas del mundo, por lo que a la acústica respecta. Las superficies curvas y afiladas, de acero inoxidable pulido, constituyen una masa danzante de volúmenes que brillan al sol entre los rascacielos. El revestimiento metálico del exterior contrasta con la calidez de la madera que predomina en las gradas y en el techo del interior del auditorio.

Situé au coeur de la ville, le foyer de l'Orchestre Philharmonique de Los Angeles est conçu pour être une des salles de concert les plus sophistiquées au monde sur le plan phonique. Les surfaces courbes et effilées en acier inoxydable poli forment un ensemble de volumes dansants qui scintillent au soleil, entre les gratte-ciels. L'habillage métallique de l'extérieur contraste avec la chaleur du bois qui prédomine sur les gradins et le plafond à l'intérieur de l'auditorium.

Ubicata nel centro della città, la sede dell'Orchestra Filarmonica di Los Angeles è stata progetta per essere una delle sale da concerto con l'acustica più sofisticata al mondo. Le superfici curve e affilate, d'acciaio inox lucidato, costituiscono un insieme di volumi danzanti che brilla al sole tra i grattacieli. Il rivestimento metallico dell'esterno contrasta con i caldi interni dell'auditorio, creati mediante l'uso predominante del legno in scalinate e soffitti.

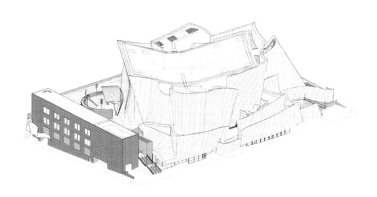

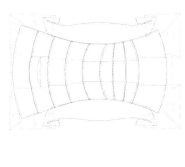

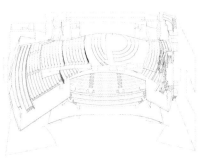

Steel stands out for being a material that remains in excellent condition over time. The architects responsible for the restoration of this building, built in 1954, could confirm this fact, after having conserved the original structure, made from steel, which they found in perfect condition. It was then clad in glass and aluminum.

Stahl ist ein sehr widerstandsfähiges und wetterfestes Material. Das konnten auch die Architekten feststellen, die dieses Gebäude aus dem Jahr 1954 restaurierten. Es war möglich, die Originalstruktur aus Stahl zu wahren, da sie sich noch in einem ausgezeichneten Zustand befand, und sie mit Glas und Aluminium zu verkleiden.

El acero destaca por ser un material que resiste en muy buenas condiciones el paso del tiempo. Los arquitectos responsables de la reforma de este edificio, construido en 1954, pudieron comprobar esta afirmación: como la estructura original realizada con acero se encontraba en plenas condiciones, a ellos les fue posible conservarla y revestirla de cristal y aluminio.

L'acier se distingue comme un matériau résistant dans de très bonnes conditions au passage du temps. Une affirmation qui a pu être vérifiée par les architectes responsables de la réforme de cet édifice construit en 1954. Ils ont conservé la structure originelle réalisée en acier, qui était en parfait état, pour la revêtir de verre et d'aluminium.

Tra le qualità dell'acciaio vi è quella di resistere in buone condizioni al passar del tempo. Ne hanno potuto avere la dimostrazione gli architetti responsabili della ristrutturazione di questo edificio costruito nel 1954, i quali hanno mantenuto la struttura originaria in acciaio che si trovava in ottime condizioni, rivestendolo di vetro e di alluminio.

The metal bridge that crosses the South Coast Plaza mall and finishes just in front of the shop, has been the inspiration for the sculptural entrance door. This perforated, polished piece of steel is surrounded by glass and has no frame. The perfect geometry transforms into curves and warm textures in the shop's interior, returning to a steel wall, again with perforations, which acts as shop window.

Die Metallbrücke, die das Einkaufszentrum South Coast Plaza überquert und genau vor dem Laden endet, war auch die Inspiration für die skulpturell gestaltete Eingangstür. Sie besteht aus glänzendem, durchbohrten Stahl, hat keinen Rahmen und ist von Glas umgeben. Die perfekte Geometrie löst sich in Kurven und warme Texturen im Inneren des Ladens auf, bis sie an einer Stahlwand wieder hergestellt wird. Auch diese hat Öffnungen, die als Ausstellungsregale dienen.

El puente metálico que atraviesa el centro comercial de South Coast Plaza y que termina justo en frente de la tienda ha inspirado la escultural puerta de la entrada. Se trata de una pieza de acero pulido que presenta perforaciones y que, rodeada solamente por cristal, no cuenta con marcos. La geometría perfecta se diluye en curvas y texturas cálidas en el interior de la tienda, hasta recomponerse en una pared de acero —otra vez con perforaciones— que sirve como escaparate.

Le pont métallique qui traverse le centre commercial de South Coast Plaza et se termine juste en face de la boutique a inspiré la porte sculpturale de l'entrée. Il s'agit d'une pièce d'acier poli perforée, sans cadre et uniquement entourée de verre. La géométrie parfaite se dilue dans les courbes et textures chaleureuses de l'intérieur de la boutique pour se recomposer sur une paroi en acier, à nouveau perforée, servant de vitrine.

Il ponte metallico che attraversa il mall di South Coast Plaza e che finisce proprio di fronte al negozio, ha ispirato la sua scultorea porta di ingresso. Si tratta di un elemento in acciaio levigato perforato, circondato soltanto da vetro e privo di intelaiature. All'interno del negozio, la perfetta geometria si dissolve in curve e texture dai toni caldi per poi ricomporsi in una parete di acciaio, anch'essa con perforazioni, che serve da vetrina.

This building is an object of design in its own right, and not merely a container for the pumps that transport sewage to the treatment plant. The steel skin that traces the station's profile, uses the metaphor of an engine. Without adding more volume than is necessary, the final shape of the building is the consequence of its function.

Dieses Gebäude wurde als ein Designobjekt an sich verstanden, und nicht als ein Container für Pumpen, die Abwasser zur Kläranlage transportieren. Seine Stahlhaut, die den Umriss der Pumpstation definiert, benutzt die Metapher eines Motors. Ohne mehr Bauteile als notwendig hinzuzufügen, ist die letztendliche Form des Gebäudes die, die sich aus seiner Funktion ergibt.

El edificio ha sido concebido como un objeto de diseño en sí, y no como un mero contenedor de las bombas que transportan las aguas residuales hacia la planta de tratamiento. La piel de acero que define el perfil de la estación alude metafóricamente a un motor. Sin agregar más volumen que el necesario, la forma final del edificio es el resultado de su función.

Cet édifice est conçu comme un objet de design, et non comme un simple container de citernes qui transportent les eaux résiduelles vers le centre d'épuration. Son enveloppe d'acier, qui définit le profil de la station, est à l'image d'un moteur. Sans ajouter plus de volume que nécessaire, la forme finale de l'édifice découle de sa fonction.

Questo edificio non è stato concepito solo per contenere le pompe che trasportano le acque reflue verso gli impianti di trattamento, ma come un autentico oggetto di design. Il suo rivestimento in pelle d'acciaio, che definisce il profilo della stazione, fa riferimento alla metafora di un motore. Senza dar origine ad un volume maggiore del necessario, la forma finale dell'edificio è il risultato diretto della sua funzione.

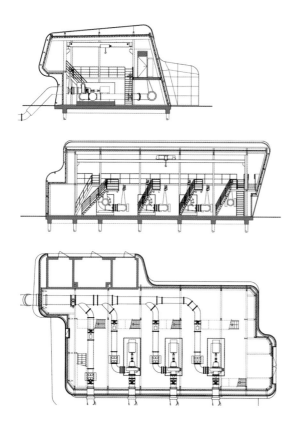

Transparency is the key to the design of this eight-story building housing the offices of the european head office of the petrol company Sabic. A large glass and steel structural facade continues across the ceiling to form a skylight that opens between the aluminum panels. As a result the light floods down the cascade of balconies in the atrium, and spreads across the steel cladding on the spiral stair and columns that reach up to the ceiling.

Transparenz diente als Inspiration für dieses achtstöckige Gebäude, in dem die europäische Zentrale der Ölgesellschaft Sabic untergebracht sind. Eine großflächige, strukturelle Fassade aus Glas und Stahl wird im Dachbereich in Form eines Dachfensters fortgesetzt, das sich zwischen Aluminiumpaneelen öffnet. Aufgrund dieser Struktur fällt das Licht über die kaskadenförmig angeordneten Balkons in das Atrium und breitet sich durch die Stahlverkleidung der Wendeltreppen und der bis zum Dach reichenden Säulen aus.

La transparencia inspira el diseño de este edificio de ocho plantas que alberga la sede europea de las oficinas de la compañía petrolera Sabic. Una amplia fachada estructural de vidrio y acero continúa en el techo en forma de un tragaluz que se abre paso entre los paneles de aluminio. Como resultado, la luz desciende por la cascada de balcones del atrio y se expande por los revestimientos de acero de la escalera de caracol y de las columnas que llegan hasta el techo.

La transparence inspire le design de cet édifice de huit étages qui abrite les bureaux de la compagnie pétrolière Sabic. Une large façade structurée de verre et d'acier se prolonge dans le toit en forme de lucarne qui se fraye un chemin entre les panneaux d'aluminium. La lumière caracole ainsi par le biais des balcons en cascade de l'atrium et se reflète dans l'habillage d'acier des escaliers en colimaçon et des colonnes allant jusqu'au plafond.

La trasparenza ispira la progettazione di questo edificio di otto piani che ospita gli uffici della compagnia petrolifera Sabic. Un'ampia facciata strutturale di vetro e acciaio si prolunga fino al tetto, formando un lucernario che si fa strada tra i pannelli di alluminio. Il risultato è una cascata di luce che zampilla tra i balconi dell'atrio e scorre lungo il rivestimento in acciaio delle scale a chiocciola e delle colonne, alte fino al soffitto.

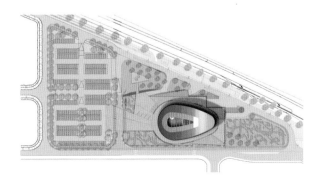

An imaginary city called Biopolis was created here to transport visitors at the Expo to the year 2022, a not-to-distant future. The buildings of this "new world" are mainly built from steel structures, a material used for cladding both interior and exterior spaces, and which offers a vision of modernity and pureness.

Der Besucher dieser Ausstellung sollte in das Jahr 2022 versetzt werden, also in die nächste Zukunft, und dazu wurde die imaginäre Stadt Biopolis geschaffen. Die Gebäude der „neuen Welt" bestehen hauptsächlich aus Stahlstrukturen, die sowohl als Außen- als auch als Innenverkleidung benutzt wurden, und die gleichzeitig modern und rein wirkt.

Con la idea de transportar al visitante de esta Expo al año 2022, un futuro muy próximo, se creó una ciudad imaginaria a la que llamaron Biopolis. Los edificios del "nuevo mundo" están creados principalmente por estructuras de acero, material que ha sido usado para revestir tanto espacios externos como internos y que nos da una sensación de modernidad y, a la vez, de pureza.

Dans l'idée de transporter le visiteur de cette Expo en l'an 2022, un futur très proche, une cité imaginaire baptisée Biopolis a été créée. Les édifices du « Nouveau monde » sont générés principalement par des structures d'acier, un matériau que nous découvrons revêtant les espaces externes comme internes et qui nous offre une vision de modernité comme de pureté.

Con l'idea di trasportare il visitatore di questa Esposizione nell'anno 2022, un futuro non molto lontano, si è creata una città immaginaria denominata Biopolis. Gli edifici del "nuovo mondo" vengono realizzati con strutture in acciaio, materiale usato per rivestire spazi esterni ed interni, e che ci dà un'immagine di modernità e una sensazione di purezza.

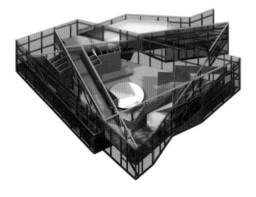

STORE

TANKSTELLE GESUNDHEIT

OB PUTZROBOTER, KÜNSTLICHES GEWEBE
ODER WELLNESS-DRAGEES:
IM HEALTHSTORE MASSGESCHNEIDERTE
LÖSUNGEN PRÜFEN.

STORE

STATION-SERVICE SANTÉ

ROBOT NETTOYEUR,
TISSU SYNTHÉTIQUE OU DRAGÉES
DE BIEN-ÊTRE: VOIR LES
SOLUTIONS SUR
MESURE AU HEALTHSTORE.

STORE

An old abandoned factory was the space chosen to install this interesting office. In an attempt to preserve the memory of the past, as well as adapting to new needs, a project was designed in which the original materials were restored and shared center-stage with today's elements such as glass and steel.

Eine alte, verlassene Fabrik war der Ort, der für dieses interessante Büro gewählt wurde. Um an die Vergangenheit zu erinnern, aber gleichzeitig moderne, gut ausgestattete Räumlichkeiten zu schaffen, restaurierte man die Originalmaterialien und verwendete gleichzeitig moderne Elemente aus Glas und Stahl.

Una antigua fábrica abandonada fue el espacio elegido para instalar esta interesante oficina. Con la voluntad de conservar la memoria del pasado, sin dejar de lado la adaptación a las nuevas necesidades, se diseñó un proyecto en el que se restauraron los materiales originales, los cuales compartían protagonismo con elementos actuales como el cristal y el acero.

Une ancienne usine abandonnée a été retenue comme espace d'installation de ce bureau intéressant. Afin de préserver la mémoire du passé tout en s'adaptant aux nouvelles nécessités, un projet a vu le jour dans le cadre duquel les matériaux d'origine ont été restaurés pour partager la vedette avec les éléments actuels, ainsi le verre et l'acier.

Una vecchia fabbrica abbandonata è stato lo spazio scelto per installarvi questo interessante ufficio. Con l'intenzione di mantenere la memoria del passato, ma adattandosi alle nuove esigenze quotidiane, si è optato per un progetto in cui i materiali originali sono restaurati e dividono la scena con elementi attuali quali il vetro e l'acciaio.

This minimalist house, designed to evoke the sea, stands alongside the esplanade of a Mediterranean city. The architect created a simple structure, a rectangular steel box, to house a small bar with an outstanding terrace, literally situated on the water in the marina. Steel and wood are the main materials used here.

Mitten an der Strandpromenade einer mediterranen Stadt befindet sich dieses minimalistische Haus. Der Architekt plante eine einfache Struktur, einen rechteckigen Kasten aus Stahl, an der die Terrasse auffällt, die sich genau über dem Wasser des Sporthafens befindet. Neben Stahl wurde als Konstruktionsmaterial hauptsächlich Holz verwendet.

En pleno paseo marítimo de una ciudad mediterránea se encuentra este edificio minimalista, que se inspira en el mar. El arquitecto creó una simple estructura, semejante a una caja rectangular de acero, en la que se sitúa un pequeño bar cuya terraza destaca por estar ubicada literalmente sobre las aguas del puerto deportivo. El acero comparte su protagonismo con la madera.

Ce minuscule édifice évoquant la mer s'invite au cœur de la promenade maritime d'une cité méditerranéenne. En le traitant comme une caisse rectangulaire en acier, l'architecte a créé une simple structure accueillant un petit bar remarquable par sa terrasse, située littéralement au-dessus des eaux du port de plaisance. L'acier comme matériau partage la vedette avec le bois.

In pieno lungomare di una città mediterranea si trova questo edificio minimalista ispirato al mare. Trattando il volume come una scatola rettangolare di acciaio, l'architetto ha creato una semplice struttura dove collocare un piccolo bar; sopra risalta la terrazza situata letteralmente sulle acque del molo da diporto. Per quanto riguarda i materiali costruttivi, l'acciaio divide la scena con il legno.

The renovation of a complex of old factories to house a large design center was to revitalize this suburban area. The restoration of one of the spaces as offices stands out among the constructions carried out. Steel was used in this project for the entrance door and the stairs that give access to the first floor.

Um ein Vorstadtviertel zu beleben, begann man mit der Restaurierung einer Reihe alter Fabriken, um dort einen Gebäudekomplex in modernem Design zu schaffen. Unter anderem wurde eines dieser Gebäude zu einem Bürohaus umgebaut. Dabei verwendete man Stahl an der Eingangstür und an der Treppe zum ersten Stockwerk.

Para revitalizar una zona suburbana se inició la renovación de un complejo de antiguas fábricas, donde se instaló un gran centro de diseño. Entre las actuaciones llevadas a cabo destaca la rehabilitación de uno de estos espacios como oficinas. Para este proyecto se utilizó el acero como material para la puerta de entrada y la escalera de acceso al primer piso.

La rénovation d'un complexe d'anciennes usines où installer un grand centre de design a été initiée afin de revitaliser une zone suburbaine. Parmi les interventions, il convient de remarquer la réhabilitation de certains de ces espaces comme bureaux. Ce projet a vu l'utilisation de l'acier comme matériau pour la porte d'entrée et l'escalier d'accès au premier niveau.

La rivitalizzazione di una zona suburbana ha avuto inizio con il rinnovamento di un vecchio complesso industriale dove installarvi un grande centro di design. Tra gli interventi portati a termine, la ristrutturazione di uno di questi spazi adibiti ad uffici. In questo progetto l'acciaio è stato impiegato come materiale nella porta d'ingresso e nella scala che dà accesso al primo piano.

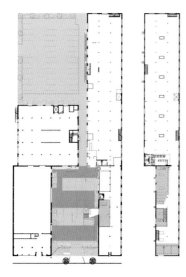

JOHNSON CHOU | TORONTO
WOMB. WORK, OFFICE, MEDIATION, BASE
Toronto, Canada | 2005

This multipurpose project was designed to make the most of the space and to be easily converted. All rooms of the house can "mutate" depending on the need at the time. The bed can be hidden giving way to a large room with steel benches, and the dining table moves in order to connect the PC. Most of the furnishings have been done in steel.

Planungsgrundlage für dieses Gebäude war es, dass der Raum sehr flexibel und maximal nutzbar sein sollte. Alle Räume des Hauses können den augenblicklichen Anforderungen entsprechend verändert werden. Das Bett wird verborgen und lässt so einen großen Saal mit Stahlbänken frei, und der Esszimmertisch wird bewegt, um den Computer anzuschließen. Die meisten der Möbel sind aus Stahl.

Este proyecto multifuncional se diseñó a partir de la voluntad de convertibilidad y aprovechamiento del espacio. Todas las habitaciones de la casa pueden "mutar" según la necesidad del momento. La cama se esconde para dar paso a una amplia sala con bancos de acero, o la mesa del comedor se mueve para poder conectar el PC. La mayoría de los muebles están realizados con acero.

Ce projet multifonctionnel a émergé de la volonté de convertibilité et de mise à profit de l'espace. Toutes les pièces de la maison peuvent « muter » selon les nécessités du moment. Le lit se cache pour laisser place à une vaste salle aux bancs d'acier, ou la table de la salle à manger bouge afin de pouvoir connecter un PC. La plupart des meubles sont réalisés en acier.

Questo progetto multifunzionale è stato disegnato partendo dalle esigenze di convertibilità e massimo sfruttamento dello spazio. Tutte le stanze della casa si possono trasformare a secondo delle necessità del momento. Il letto si nasconde per lasciare spazio ad un'ampia sala con delle panche in acciaio, o il tavolo dalla sala da pranzo si sposta per poter collegare il computer. La maggior parte dei mobili sono realizzati in acciaio.

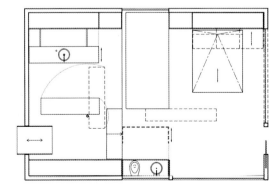

JOHNSON CHOU | TORONTO
YOLLES RESIDENCE
Toronto, Canada | 2005

To achieve this loft the first idea was to eliminate the non structural walls and replace them by large sliding doors. Among these new dividing forms is the stainless steel door that separates the bedroom from the living area. This material is found in other areas of the house such as in the original dressing room, which acts as a corridor to the toilet.

Beim Umbau dieses Lofts entfernte man zuerst die nicht tragenden Mauern und ersetzte sie durch große Schiebetüren. Unter diesen neuen Abtrennungen fällt eine Tür aus Edelstahl auf, die das Schlafzimmer vom Wohnbereich abtrennt. Dieses Material wurde auch in anderen Bereichen der Wohnung verwendet, so zum Beispiel an dem separaten Toilettentisch, der gleichzeitig einen Durchgang zur Toilette entstehen lässt.

Para llevar a cabo este loft, la primera idea fue la de eliminar los muros no estructurales y sustituirlos por grandes puertas correderas. Entre estas nuevas formas divisorias destaca la puerta de acero inoxidable que separa el dormitorio de la zona de estar. Encontramos el acero en otros espacios y elementos de la casa como el original tocador independiente que sirve de pasillo hacia el lavabo.

Pour matérialiser ce loft, la première idée fut d'éliminer les murs non porteurs afin de leur substituer de grandes portes coulissantes. Parmi ces nouvelles formes de division, l'on remarque la porte en acier inoxydable qui sépare la chambre de la salle de séjour. Ce matériau se rencontre également dans d'autres espaces de la maison, ainsi le cabinet de toilette indépendant servant de couloir jusqu'au lavabo.

L'idea primordiale per la realizzazione di questo loft è stata quella di eliminare le pareti non portanti e sostituirle con delle porte scorrevoli. Tra questi nuovi elementi divisori spicca la porta in acciaio inossidabile che separa la camera da letto dalla zona soggiorno. Tra gli altri spazi della casa dove è presente l'acciaio, vi è l'originale toilette indipendente che serve da corridoio verso il bagno.

JOSÉ MARÍA LÓPEZ & MANUEL RÓDENAS | MURCIA
LEISURE PAVILION
Manga del Mar Menor, Spain | 2005

For this sea-side, beach pavilion the architects opted for a rectangular steel structure, to which methacry late panels were applied as walls In the green and blue tones of the Mediterranean. The project is characterized by the sensation of lightness and expectancy, an idea enhanced by the location.

Für diesen Pavillon am Strand ganz nah am Meer wählten die Architekten eine rechteckige Stahlstruktur, die sie mit Metacrylatplatten in Grün- und Blautönen schlossen, Farbtöne, die sehr typisch für Mittelmeerregionen sind. Die Konstruktion wirkt sehr leicht und fast zufällig, eine Wirkung, die durch den besonderen Standort noch verstärkt wirkt.

Para este pabellón de playa, situado muy cerca del mar, los arquitectos optaron por una estructura rectangular de acero, a la que aplicaron a modo de cerramientos paneles de metacrilato de color en los tonos verdes y azules propios del Mediterráneo. Este proyecto se caracteriza por la sensación de ligereza y provisionalidad, idea que se acentúa por su ubicación.

Pour ce pavillon de plage, très proche de la mer, les architectes ont opté pour une structure rectangulaire en acier sur laquelle ils ont appliqué pour la clore des panneaux de méthacrylate colorés aux tons verts et bleus, proprement méditerranéens. Ce projet se caractérise par la sensation de légèreté et d'éventualité, une idée rehaussée par le lieu.

Per questo padiglione marittimo, situato molto vicino al mare, gli architetti hanno optato per una struttura rettangolare in acciaio, a cui sono stati applicati, a guisa di chiusura, dei pannelli in metacrilato colorato nei toni verde ed azzurro, propri del Mediterraneo. Il progetto si caratterizza per la sensazione di leggerezza e provvisorietà, idea che viene accentuata dalla sua ubicazione.

JUN AOKI | TOKYO
WHITE CHAPEL
Osaka, Japan | 2006

The curtain of interlinked steel rings acts as a mesh that lends intimacy to the interior of the chapel. This metallic skin allows a generous amount of natural light to penetrate the interior during the day, and at night the building becomes a lantern that radiates light to the outside. In keeping with the building's character, the steel helps to give the composition an almost ethereal nature.

Die Gardine aus miteinander verbundenen Stahlringen wirkt wie ein Flechtwerk, das in seinem geschütz-ten Inneren eine Kapelle beherbergt. Diese Haut aus Metall lässt das Tageslicht großzügig in die Räume strömen und das Gebäude nachts wie eine Laterne wirken, die Licht nach außen strahlt. Der verwende-te Stahl macht die Konstruktion fast immateriell, wodurch der religiöse Charakter des Gebäudes noch vertieft wird.

La cortina de argollas de acero entrelazadas funcionan como un entramado que guarda la intimidad del interior de la capilla. Esta piel metálica permite que, durante el día, la luz natural penetre en el recinto de manera generosa, y que, durante la noche, la edificación se transforme en una linterna que irradia la luz hacia el exterior. Acorde con el carácter del edificio, el acero ayuda a dar a la composición una natu-raleza casi incorpórea.

Le rideau d'anneaux d'acier entrelacés joue le rôle d'un lattis préservant l'intimité intérieure de la chapelle. Cette enveloppe métallique laisse la lumière naturelle entrer à flots dans l'enceinte durant le jour, et, la nuit tombée, métamorphose l'édifice en une lanterne qui irradie la lumière vers l'extérieur. En harmonie avec la nature de l'édifice, l'acier confère à la composition un aspect naturel qui frise l'immatérialité.

La cortina di anelli d'acciaio intrecciati forma una trama che mantiene l'intimità all'interno della cappel-la. Questa pelle metallica, che non rappresenta un ostacolo alla penetrazione di abbondante luce natu-rale durante il giorno, di notte dà alla struttura le sembianze di una lanterna che sprigiona luce verso l'esterno. Accordandosi perfettamente al carattere dell'edificio, l'acciaio fa sì che la composizione assu-ma una natura quasi incorporea.

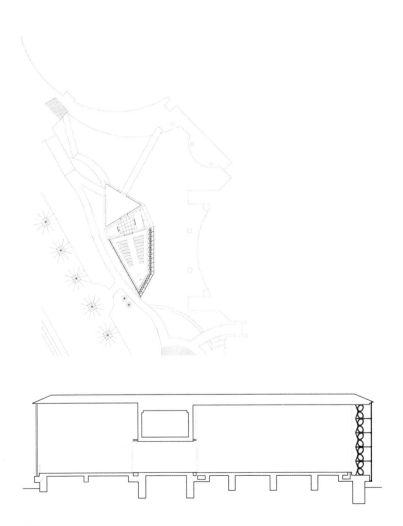

KAZUHIKO OISHI ARCHITECTURE ATELIER | FUKUOKA
FABRIC WALL RESIDENCE
Tokyo, Japan | 2005

A steel structure is the outstanding constructive feature that allowed for the creation of this cubic home of pure lines. The metal skeleton allows the walls of the house to be made from double-glazed sheets, which incorporate a fabric that allows the interior to either be illuminated or not depending on the desired level of intimacy.

Ein Stahlstruktur ist das wichtigste konstruktive Merkmal dieses würfelförmigen Gebäudes mit klaren Linien. Das Metallskelett macht es möglich, dass die Wände des Hauses aus doppeltem Glas bestehen, in deren Inneren ein Gewebe angebracht wurde, so dass das Innere des Hauses beleuchtet, aber vor Blicken abgeschirmt ist.

Una estructura de acero es la característica constructiva que posibilita la creación de esta vivienda cúbica y de líneas puras. El esqueleto metálico permite que las paredes de la vivienda estén creadas a partir de un doble cristal glaseado, el cual incluye, dentro de sus capas, una tela que permite iluminar el interior de la casa, a la vez que sirve para dar intimidad.

Una structure d'acier est la caractéristique architecturale rendant possible la genèse de cette demeure cubique aux lignes pures. Le squelette métallique permet la création des murs de la demeure à partir d'un double vitrage, des parois dont les couches incluent une toile permettant d'illuminer l'intérieur de la maison tout en préservant l'intimité.

Un'ossatura in acciaio è l'elemento costruttivo che ha reso possibile la creazione di questa abitazione dalla forma cubica e linee pure. L'armatura metallica permette che le pareti della casa vengano create a partire da un doppio vetro glassato; all'interno di questo, tra i suoi strati, è stata inserita una tela che permette di illuminare l'interno della casa e che serve contemporaneamente a creare un po' di privacy.

LAB ARCHITECTURE STUDIO | LONDON
FEDERATION SQUARE
Melbourne, Australia | 2006

A large urban complex has been built in Melbourne formed by interesting buildings and used for both cultural and commercial spaces. The projects that make up this "new city" are noteworthy for their use of highly advanced materials and technologies. Steel is present in a large part of the structures, allowing the creation of large spaces.

In Melbourne errichtete man eine große, interessant gestaltete Gebäudegruppe, die sowohl kulturellen als auch kommerziellen Zwecken dient. Bei dieser „neuen Stadt" verwendete man die fortschrittlichsten Materialien und Technologien. Ein großer Teil der Strukturen sind aus Stahl, so dass man große Räume schaffen konnte.

En Melbourne se ha construido un gran complejo urbanístico formado por interesantes edificios destinados tanto a espacios culturales como comerciales. Los proyectos que conforman esta "nueva ciudad" destacan por la utilización de los más avanzados materiales y de las tecnologías punteras. El acero está presente en gran parte de las estructuras, permitiendo la creación de grandes espacios.

Melbourne a vu la construction d'un vaste complexe urbanistique formé d'immeubles intéressants destinés aux activités culturelles et commerciales. Les projets formant cette « nouvelle ville » se distinguent par l'emploi des matériaux les plus avancés et de technologies de pointe. L'acier est présent dans une grande partie des structures, permettant de générer de vastes espaces.

A Melbourne è stato costruito un grande complesso urbanistico formato da interessanti edifici da adibire sia ad usi culturali che commerciali. I progetti che costituiscono questa "nuova città" si fanno notare per l'utilizzo dei più avanzati materiali e delle tecnologie più all'avanguardia. L'acciaio, presente in gran parte delle strutture, consente la creazione di grandi spazi.

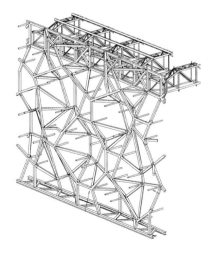

M2-NAKATSUJI ARCHITECT ATELIER | TOKYO
F HOUSE
Mukonoso, Japan | 2004

The steel panels that cover the main façade and roof of this cubic house are strategically positioned so that the pieces are not perfectly joined. This solution allows the entry of small rays of light into the home, luminous lines, which give the interior an original decorative and artistic feature.

Die Stahlplatten an der Hauptfassade und an dem Dach dieses würfelförmigen Hauses sind mit Absicht so verlegt, dass sie nicht perfekt zusammenpassen. So gelangen kleine Lichtstrahlen ins Haus, Lichtlinien, die im Inneren wie originelle Dekorationselemente oder Kunstobjekte behandelt werden.

Las placas de acero que recubren la fachada principal y la cubierta de esta casa cúbica están colocadas de manera estratégica para que las piezas no queden perfectamente unidas. Esta solución permite la entrada en la vivienda de pequeños rayos de luz, líneas luminosas que en el interior están tratadas a modo de originales elementos decorativos o artísticos.

Les plaques d'acier qui recouvrent la façade principale et le toit de cette maison cubique sont disposés de manière stratégique afin que les pièces ne soient pas parfaitement unies. Cette solution permet de laisser pénétrer de minuscules rayons de lumière dans la demeure, des lignes lumineuses qui sont traitées à l'intérieur comme des éléments décoratifs originaux voire artistiques.

Le lastre di acciaio che rivestono la facciata principale e la copertura di questa casa a forma di cubo sono disposte in maniera strategica affinché i vari pezzi non combacino alla perfezione. Questa soluzione consente il passaggio nell'abitazione di piccoli raggi di luce, linee luminose che aiutano a dare un tocco artistico e decorativo all'ambiente interno.

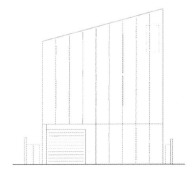

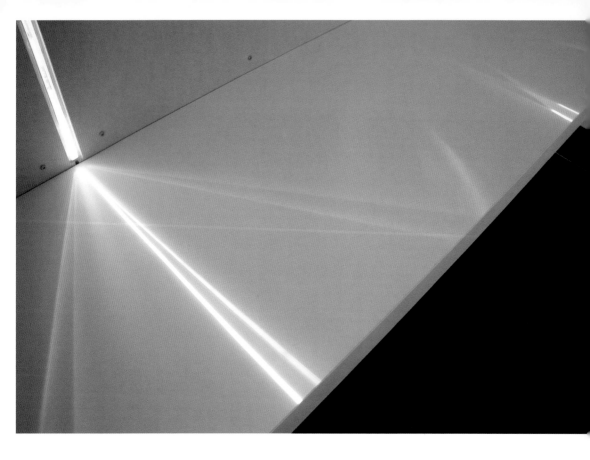

MAP ARQUITECTOS / JOSEP LLUÍS MATEO | BARCELONA
CCIB FORUM
Barcelona, Spain | 2004

This Conference Center was designed to accommodate a maximum of 18,000 people who attended the
conferences that took place in the city. Its impressive façade, clad in steel panels, stands out for the design
of these constructive elements, since each metal piece has been perforated in a different way, giving the
project an irregular image.

Das Kongresszentrum wurde für maximal 18 000 Menschen entworfen, die zu den Kongressen erwartet
werden, die in der Stadt stattfinden. Die beeindruckende Fassade ist mit Stahlplatten verkleidet und fällt
vor allem durch die Gestaltung dieser Konstruktionselemente auf. Jedes Metallteil wurde anders durch-
bohrt, so dass das Gesamtbild recht unregelmäßig ist.

El Centro de Convenciones fue ideado para acoger hasta 18 000 participantes de los congresos que se
celebran en la ciudad. Su impresionante fachada, recubierta por planchas de acero, destaca por el diseño de estos elementos constructivos, ya que cada pieza metálica ha sido perforada de distinta manera,
lo que da una imagen irregular al proyecto.

Le Palais des Congrès a été pensé pour accueillir jusqu'à 18 000 participants aux conventions organi-
sées dans la ville. Sa façade impressionnante, couverte de planches d'acier, se distingue par le design
de ces éléments de construction. En effet, chaque pièce a été perforée de manière différente pour
conférer une image irrégulière au projet.

Il Centro di Convenzioni è stato ideato per accogliere un massimo di 18 000 persone partecipanti ai vari
congressi che si tengono nella città. La sua imponente facciata, rivestita da lastre di acciaio, risalta per
il disegno di questi elementi costruttivi, visto che ogni singolo pezzo metallico è stato perforato in maniera distinta, dando così un'immagine irregolare al progetto.

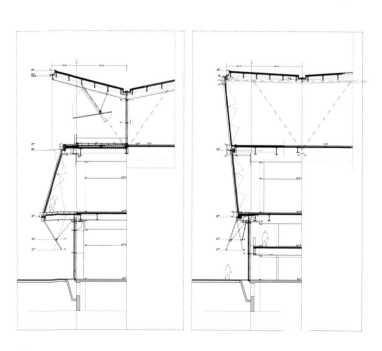

MASSIMILIANO FUKSAS | ROME
NEW MILAN TRADE FAIR
Milan, Italy | 2005

Arranged along a central axis, the installations that hold the offices, exhibition areas and toilets for Milan's new trade fair venue are spread across a series of stages dominated by water, grass and concrete. The steel sheets that clad the pavilion walls reflect the surroundings. Above this, lying unseen, the undulating glass roof stretches out, laminated with a rhomboidal steel structure, which draws on the natural shapes of craters, sand dunes and tornados.

Das neue Messegelände von Mailand erstreckt sich entlang einer zentralen Achse, an der die Bürogebäude, die Ausstellungshallen und die verschiedenen Infrastruktureinrichtungen liegen. Wasser, Rasen und Beton bestimmen das Bild. Die Stahlplatten, mit denen die Wände der Ausstellungshallen verkleidet sind, reflektieren die Umgebung. Darüber schwebt gleich einem Schleier ein gewelltes Dach aus gewalztem Glas mit einer rhomboidförmigen Stahlstruktur, die Formen der Natur wie Krater, Dünen und Wirbelstürme imitiert.

Dispuestas a lo largo de un eje central, las instalaciones, que albergan las oficinas, las áreas de exhibición y los servicios de la nueva feria de Milán, recorren diversos escenarios dominados por el agua, el césped y el hormigón. Las placas de acero que revisten las paredes de los pabellones reflejan el entorno. Por encima, cual velo, se extiende un techo ondulante de cristal laminado, que cuenta con una estructura compuesta por rombos de acero. El techo toma prestado de la naturaleza las formas de los cráteres, las dunas y los dinámicos tornados.

Disposées le long d'un axe central, les installations qui abritent les bureaux, les zones d'exposition et les services de la nouvelle foire de Milan traversent diverses mises en scène dominées par l'eau, la pelouse et le béton. Les environs se reflètent dans les plaques d'acier qui habillent les murs des pavillons. En outre, à l'image d'un voile, un toit ondulant en verre laminé, se prolonge par une structure rhomboïde d'acier qui empreinte à la nature ses formes de cratères, dunes et tornades fougueuses.

Disposte lungo un'asse centrale, le costruzioni che ospitano gli uffici, le aree espositive e i servizi della nuova fiera di Milano percorrono diversi scenari dominati da acqua, prato e cemento. Le lastre d'acciaio che rivestono le pareti dei padiglioni riflettono l'ambiente circostante. Nella parte superiore, il tetto si estende come un velo ondulato di cristallo laminato, con una struttura d'acciaio romboidale, che prende in prestito dalla natura le forme dei crateri, delle dune e di vorticosi tornado.

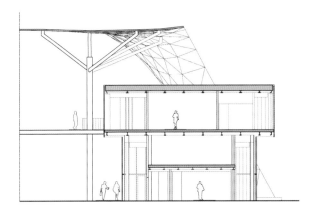

OLSON SUNDBERG KUNDIG ALLEN ARCHITECTS | SEATTLE
CHICKEN POINT CABIN
Idaho, United States | 2003

This original house was designed in an attempt to integrate this small building with its picturesque surroundings. The extremely high steel door at the entrance welcomes us into a space where we are met by an enormous chimney of unpolished steel, which acts as both a column and a way of dividing the space.

Das kleine, originelle Gebäude sollte sich in die wunderschöne Landschaft integrieren, die es umgibt. Eine außergewöhnlich hohe Eingangstür aus Stahl lässt uns in einem Raum, der von einem enormen Kamin aus mattem Stahl beherrscht wird. Dieses Konstruktionselement dient gleichzeitig als Säule und als den Raum ordnendes Element.

Esta original vivienda ha sido diseñada con el objeto de lograr su integración en el bello paisaje que la rodea. La altísima puerta principal, realizada con acero, nos invita a adentrarnos en un espacio en el que destaca una enorme chimenea de acero no pulido, elemento que también tiene la función de columna y de distribuidor del espacio.

Cette demeure originale a été pensée avec la volonté d'intégrer ce petit édifice au cœur du superbe paysage environnant. Très haute, la porte d'entrée réalisée en acier nous invite à nous aventurer dans un espace où se détache une énorme cheminée fabriquée en acier non poli, un élément qui revêt également la fonction de colonne et de distributeur de l'espace.

Questa originale abitazione è stata disegnata partendo dalla volontà di far integrare questo piccolo edificio nel bel paesaggio che lo circonda. L'altissima porta di ingresso, realizzata in acciaio, ci invita ad addentrarci in uno spazio dove risalta un enorme camino in acciaio non levigato, elemento che assolve la funzione di colonna e di distributore dello spazio.

The steel structure contained within a large black box emulates a bone cell with cavities that hold the various, visually connected rooms. This irregular three-dimensional mesh stretches and molds, adapting to the building's existing architecture and covering the terrace. It is formed from almost four hundred laser-cut, folded steel pieces. At night, from the outside, the structure appears as a bizarre lamp of different colors, while during the day it becomes a vivid blue volume with irregular sides.

Die Stahlstruktur in einem großen schwarzen Kasten imitiert eine Knochenzelle voller Höhlungen, in denen sich verschiedene, visuell miteinander verbundene Räume befinden. Es handelt sich um ein unregelmäßiges, dreidimensionales Netz, das auseinandergezogen und geformt wurde, um die bereits bestehende Architektur des Gebäudes anzupassen und die Terrasse zu überdachen. Dieses Netz besteht aus fast vierhundert lasergeschnittenen und gefalteten Stahlteilen. Bei Nacht sieht die Struktur von außen wie eine seltsame, bunte Lampe aus, tagsüber nimmt sie eine intensiv blaue Farbe mit unregelmäßigen Facetten an.

La estructura de acero, contenida en una gran caja negra, emula una célula ósea que da lugar a cavidades en las que se reparten distintos ambientes conectados visualmente. Se trata de una malla tridimensional, irregular, estirada y moldeada que se adapta a la arquitectura existente del edificio y cubre el espacio de la terraza. Esta malla está formada por casi cuatrocientas piezas de acero cortadas con láser y plegadas. Desde el exterior, la estructura se ve por la noche como una extraña lámpara de colores variables, mientras que a la luz del día se convierte en un volumen azul intenso con facetas irregulares.

La structure d'acier, insérée dans une grande cage noire, imite une cellule osseuse créant des cavités où se répartissent divers univers reliés visuellement entre eux. Elle prend la forme d'un filet de mailles tridimensionnel irrégulier, étiré et façonné pour s'adapter à l'architecture existante de l'édifice et couvrir toute la terrasse. Ce filet est constitué d'environ quatre cent morceaux d'acier découpés au laser et pliés. De l'extérieur, la nuit tombée, la structure revêt l'allure d'une étrange lampe aux couleurs fluctuantes, pour se métamorphoser, à la lumière du jour, en un volume aux facettes irrégulières, d'un bleu intense.

La struttura d'acciaio, contenuta in una grande scatola nera, emula una cellula ossea dotata di varie cavità dove trovano spazio diversi ambienti, visivamente collegati tra loro. Si tratta di una maglia tridimensionale irregolare, allungata e modellata per adattarsi all'architettura preesistente dell'edificio e coprire lo spazio della terrazza. La maglia è formata da quasi quattrocento pezzi d'acciaio tagliati col laser e piegati. Dall'esterno, di notte la struttura assume l'aspetto di una bizzarra lampada dai colori cangianti, mentre alla luce del giorno si trasforma in un volume blu intenso con sfaccettature irregolari.

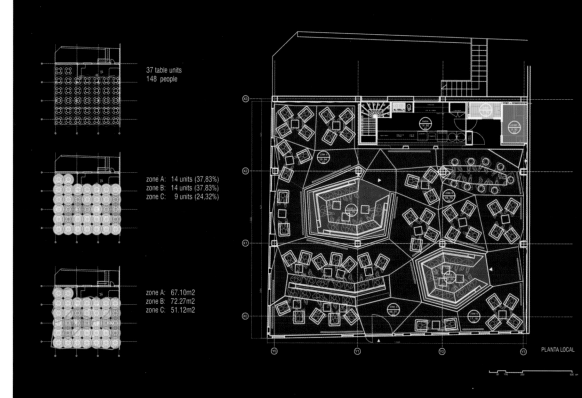

37 table units
148 people

zone A: 14 units (37,83%)
zone B: 14 units (37,83%)
zone C: 9 units (24,32%)

zone A: 67.10m2
zone B: 72.27m2
zone C: 51.12m2

PLANTA LOCAL

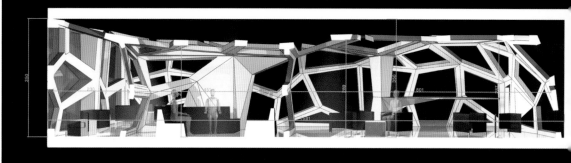

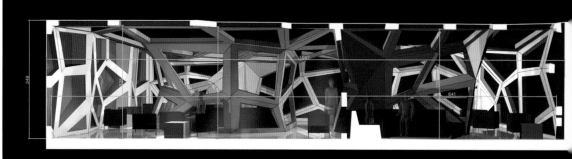

This building's organic volumes use the exterior atmospheric agents to save energy and allow the construction to operate in a sustainable manner. The triple-bodied elliptical, open floor plan runs from north to south to optimize the lighting and natural ventilation, while the courtyards act as acoustic cushioning and the paneled skin protects the work posts from the sunlight.

Die organioohen Formen dieses Gebäudes benutzen äußere, atmosphärische Mittel, um Energie zu spa ren und cinc umweltgerechte Funktion zu garantieren. Der ellipsenförmige und offene Grundriss mit einem dreifachen Körper ist in Nord Süd-Richtung ausgerichtet, um den Lichteinfall und die natürliche Belüftung zu optimieren. Die Innenhöfe dämpfen den Lärm und die Paneele der Verkleidung schützen die Arbeitsplätze vor dem Sonnenlicht.

La volumetría orgánica del edificio utiliza los agentes exteriores atmosféricos en beneficio de un mayor ahorro de energía y un funcionamiento sostenible. La planta elíptica y abierta en forma de triple cuerpo está orientada en sentido Norte-Sur para optimizar la iluminación y la ventilación natural, en tanto que los patios actúan como colchones acústicos y los paneles preservan los puestos de trabajo de la radiación solar.

La volumétrie organique de cet édifice utilise les agents extérieurs atmosphériques pour réaliser un gain d'énergie significatif et offrir un fonctionnement durable. Le rez-de-chaussée elliptique et ouvert, formé de trois corps, suit une orientation nord-sud pour optimiser l'éclairage et la ventilation naturelle. Les patios, à leur tour, jouent le rôle de coussins phoniques et l'habillage, fait de panneaux, préserve les postes de travail du rayonnement solaire.

La volumetria organica di questo edificio utilizza gli agenti atmosferici esterni per ottenere un maggior risparmio energetico e garantire un funzionamento sostenibile. La pianta ellittica, aperta in forma di triplo corpo, è orientata da nord verso sud per ottimizzare l'illuminazione e la ventilazione naturale, mentre i cortili svolgono la funzione d'isolanti acustici, con un rivestimento di pannelli che protegge le postazioni di lavoro dalle radiazioni solari.

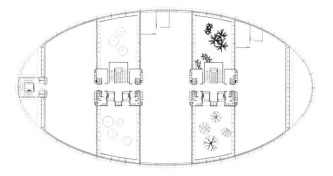

This tiny bathroom pavilion merges with its forest landscape following the curve of the river. Its volumes house changing rooms, showers, toilets and a drinks kiosk, all with stainless steel finishes to prevent damage from vandals. Daylight filters into the interior spaces through the glass pane positioned between the sheets of perforated steel.

Dieser winzige Badepavillon mitten im Wald wirkt wie eine landschaftliche Skulptur, die der Kurve des beschiffbaren Flusses folgt. In seinen Formen sind Umkleideräume, Duschen, Toiletten und ein Getränkestand untergebracht, alles aus beständigem Edelstahl. Das Tageslicht filtert sich durch Glasscheiben, die zwischen den gelöcherten Stahlplatten angebracht sind, ins Innere.

Este diminuto pabellón de baño, que, ubicado en el interior de un bosque, parece una escultura, sigue la curva de un río navegable. Sus volúmenes albergan vestuarios, duchas, lavabos y un quiosco de bebidas con acabados de acero inoxidable para resistir el vandalismo. En los espacios interiores, la luz del día se filtra a través del cristal colocado entre las planchas de acero perforado.

Ce minuscule pavillon de bain, inséré dans un écrin boisé, est à l'image d'une sculpture paysagée qui suit les courbes d'un fleuve navigable. Au coeur de ses volumes, il abrite les vestiaires, douches, toilettes et un kiosque à boissons aux finitions en acier inoxydable pour résister au vandalisme. Dans les espaces intérieurs, la lumière du jour est tamisée par le verre placé entre les planches d'acier perforé.

Questo piccolo padiglione di servizi in mezzo al bosco sembra una scultura paesaggistica che segue la curva di un fiume navigabile. I suoi volumi ospitano spogliatoi, docce, toilette e un chiosco per le bibite con finiture in acciaio inox, come protezione contro atti vandalici. Negli spazi interni, la luce del giorno penetra attraverso il vetro collocato tra le lastre d'acciaio perforato.

RENZO PIANO BUILDING WORKSHOP | GENOA
PAUL KLEE ZENTRUM
Berne, Switzerland | 2006

The donation of a large number of pieces from artist Paul Klee made the foundation of the same name consider the need to design a modern museum. As well as being an exhibition center, it also acts as a restoration workshop and auditorium. A clear idea of the content allowed the creation of this spectacular steel building, formed from three volumes that literally surge from the earth.

Da der Stiftung Paul Klee eine große Zahl an Werken des Künstlers gespendet wurden, sah man sich vor die Notwendigkeit gestellt, ein modernes Museum zu einzurichten. Außer dem Ausstellungssaal sollte es auch eine Restaurationswerkstatt oder einen Konzertsaal geben. Da man eine klare Vorstellung davon hatte, was dieses Gebäude enthalten sollte, entstand ein auffallender Stahlbau, der aus drei Körpern besteht, die der Erde zu entspringen scheinen.

La donación de un gran número de obras del artista Paul Klee hizo que la fundación que lleva su nombre se planteara la necesidad de diseñar un moderno museo. A su función como centro expositivo se debían sumar otras como la de taller de restauración o auditorio. Una clara idea sobre el contenido permitió la creación de este espectacular edificio de acero, formado por tres volúmenes que surgen literalmente de la tierra.

La donation de nombreuses œuvres de l'artiste Paul Klee a conduit la fondation portant son nom à envisager la nécessité de créer un musée moderne. À sa vocation de centre d'exposition devaient s'ajouter d'autres fonctions, ainsi un atelier de restauration ou un auditorium. Une idée claire du contenu a permis de créer cet édifice spectaculaire en acier, formé de trois volumes qui surgissent littéralement de terre.

La donazione di un gran numero di opere del pittore Paul Klee ha fatto sì che l'omonima fondazione decidesse di costruire un moderno museo dove radunarle. Oltre ad assolvere la funzione espositiva, l'edificio doveva fungere anche da laboratorio di restauro o auditorio. Tre morbide ma possenti onde di vetro e di acciaio che si insinuano tra le colline sono la struttura portante di questo edificio progettato dal rinomato architetto genovese Renzo Piano.

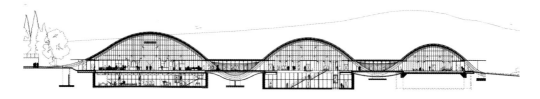

Metal has played a decisive role in the rejuvenation of this traditional seaside hotel. While the facade's new bronze skin continues towards the interior, eventually becoming the bar stools, steel defines the enormous ring of the reception area, acting as the front desk. This metal then extends to the interior columns and walls of the communal spaces of this ultra-modern hotel, and culminates with decorative details in the bedrooms.

Metall spielte eine entscheidende Rolle bei der Modernisierung dieses traditionellen Hotels an der Küste. Die neue Bronzehaut der Fassade dringt bis ins Innere, wo sie sich in Barhocker verwandelt, und das Material Stahl definiert den riesigen Ring, der den Empfangsbereich und die Rezeption aufnimmt. Dieses Metall greift dann auf die Säulen und Wände der hochmodernen Gesellschaftsräume des Hotels über, und ist schließlich noch in den dekorativen Elementen auf den Zimmern zu finden.

El metal ha jugado un rol decisivo en el rejuvenecimiento de este tradicional *resort* costero. En tanto que la nueva piel de bronce de la fachada se cuela hacia el interior del edificio y termina en los asientos del bar, el acero define el enorme anillo que ocupa la recepción y que hace de mostrador. Este metal también se encuentra en las columnas y en las paredes interiores de los espacios comunes de este hotel de última generación, así como en ciertos detalles decorativos de las habitaciones.

Le métal a joué un rôle décisif dans la rénovation de cet hôtel côtier traditionnel. Alors que la nouvelle enveloppe de bronze de la façade se glisse à l'intérieur de l'édifice pour s'achever sur les sièges du bar, l'acier définit l'immense anneau qui occupe la réception et sert de comptoir. Ce métal s'étend ensuite aux colonnes et murs intérieurs des espaces communs de cet hôtel de dernier cri, pour finir en apothéose dans les détails décoratifs des chambres.

Il metallo ha giocato un ruolo decisivo nel dare un'aria più giovanile a questo tradizionale hotel costiero. Mentre la nuova pelle di bronzo della facciata si insinua nell'edificio fino a raggiungere i sedili del bar, l'acciaio dà forma all'enorme anello che occupa la reception e che funge da bancone. Il suo uso si estende inoltre alle colonne e alle pareti interne degli spazi comuni di questo hotel d'ultima generazione, culminando nei dettagli decorativi delle stanze.

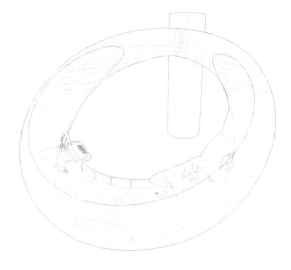

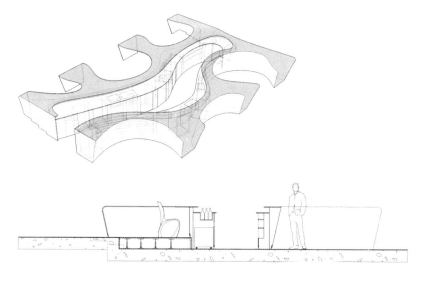

SANTA-RITA ARQUITECTOS / JOÃO SANTA-RITA | LISBON
RESTAURANT IN OEIRAS
Lisbon, Portugal | 2005

The extension of a building of swimming pools located on the Atlantic coast, offered the opportunity to install a new restaurant. To take weight from the structure of the former construction, lighter materials were chosen, such as metal and wood. A structure of painted steel defines a large interior space and frames the beautiful ocean backdrop.

Durch die Erweiterung dieses Schwimmbades an der Atlantikküste ergab sich die Möglichkeit, ein neues Restaurant zu schaffen. Um die bereits vorhandene Struktur zu entlasten, entschied man sich für leichtere Materialien wie Metall und Holz. Eine gestrichene Stahlstruktur definiert einen großen inneren Raum und umrahmt die wunderschöne Ozeanlandschaft.

La ampliación de un edificio de piscinas situado en la costa atlántica dio la oportunidad de instalar un nuevo restaurante. Para descargar la estructura de la antigua construcción, se eligieron materiales menos pesados, como el metal y la madera. La estructura de acero pintado sirve para definir un amplio espacio interior, a la vez que enmarca el bello paisaje del océano.

L'extension d'un édifice de piscines situé sur la côte Atlantique a donné l'occasion d'installer un nouveau restaurant. Afin de décharger la structure de l'ancienne construction, des éléments moins lourds, ainsi le métal et le bois, ont été retenus. La structure d'acier peint sert à définir un vaste espace intérieur tout en encadrant le magnifique paysage océanique.

L'ampliamento di un edificio di piscine situato nella costa atlantica ha offerto la possibilità di installare un nuovo ristorante. Per alleggerire la struttura dell'antica costruzione, sono stati scelti materiali meno pesanti come il metallo e il legno. Una struttura in acciaio dipinto che serve per definire un ampio spazio interno e al contempo fa da cornice all'incantevole paesaggio dell'oceano.

SHUHEI ENDO ARCHITECT INSTITUTE | OSAKA
ROOFTECTURE O-K
Kyoto, Japan | 2005

Steel is a material, which, despite its high level of resistance, is recognized for its ductility, allowing the design of interesting constructions where the architect can create and combine original forms. This small building is an example, where the curved roof lends the project movement.

Stahl ist ein Material, das trotz seiner hohen Widerstandsfähigkeit formbar ist und deshalb interessante Konstruktionen möglich macht, bei denen der Architekt mit originellen Formen spielen kann. Ein Beispiel dafür ist dieses kleine Gebäude mit dem gekrümmten Dach, das ein bewegtes Gesamtbild entstehen lässt.

El acero es un material que, a pesar de su gran resistencia, destaca por su ductilidad, característica que posibilita el diseño de interesantes construcciones en las que el arquitecto puede jugar con la creación de originales formas. Un ejemplo de ello es este pequeño edificio en el que la cubierta curva da movimiento al proyecto.

L'acier est un matériau qui, en dépit de sa grande résistance est hautement ductile, une caractéristique rendant possible le design de constructions intéressantes où l'architecte peut jouer avec la création de formes originales. Ce petit édifice, dont le toit courbe confère son mouvement au projet, en est un exemple.

Nonostante la sua grande resistenza, l'acciaio è un materiale che spicca per la sua duttilità, caratteristica che consente il disegno di singolari costruzioni dove l'architetto può giocare con la creazione di forme originali. Ne è la prova questo piccolo edificio dove la copertura curva imprime movimento al progetto.

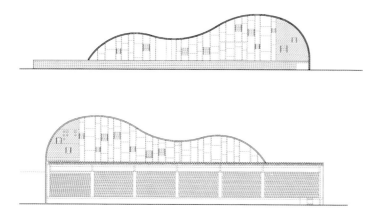

SHUHEI ENDO ARCHITECT INSTITUTE | OSAKA
ROOFTECTURE S
Kobe, Japan | 2005

This two-story home was designed on a small, narrow and irregular site, and occupies a particularly pre-carious position on the slopes of a mountain. The roof of the house, made from galvanized steel, is an expressionist design with accentuated sharp forms allowing the project to adapt perfectly to the terrain and its surroundings.

Auf einem winzigen, schmalen und sehr unregelmäßigen Grundstück errichtete man dieses kleine, zwei-stöckige Haus, das vor allem durch die schwierige Lage an einem Berghang auffällt. Das Dach des Hau-ses aus verzinktem Stahl zeigt sich in expressionistischem Design mit betont spitzen Formen, durch die das Gebäude sich perfekt an das Grundstück und die Umgebung anpasst.

En un terreno de reducidas dimensiones, estrecho y muy irregular, se diseñó esta pequeña vivienda de dos plantas, en la que destaca su difícil situación en la ladera de la montaña. La cubierta de la casa, rea-lizada con acero galvanizado, presenta un diseño expresionista con marcadas formas agudas que con-siguen que el proyecto se adapte perfectamente al terreno y a su entorno.

Ce terrain petit, étroit et très irrégulier accueille une petite demeure de deux étages conçue sur un emplacement à flanc de montagne remarquable par sa difficulté. Le toit de la maison, en acier galva-nisé, est un design expressionniste aux formes aiguës prononcées qui matérialisent un projet s'adaptant parfaitement au terrain et à son cadre.

In un terreno di ridotte dimensioni, stretto e irregolare, è stata disegnata questa piccola abitazione a due piani che sorprende per la sua disagevole ubicazione sul fianco di un montagna. La copertura della casa, realizzata in acciaio galvanizzato, è un disegno espressionista dalle marcate forme acute che contribui-scono al perfetto adattamento del progetto al terreno e all'ambiente circostante.

For this building, designed for the sale of cars, a combination of volumes was chosen which are connected via unusual roofs that adapt to the different modules. To achieve this sober and original project, the main material used was steel, whose resistance allows the roofs to be used as display platforms for the cars.

Bei diesem Autohaus spielten die Planer mit verschiedenen Körpern, die durch originelle Dächer, die sich an die verschiedenen Baukörper anpassen, verbunden sind. Um dieses schlichte und gleichzeitig außergewöhnliche Gebäude zu konstruieren benutzte man hauptsächlich Stahl, dessen Widerstandskraft es möglich macht, die Dächer als Schaufenster für die Autos zu benutzen.

En la construcción de este edificio destinado a la venta de coches se eligió jugar con diversos volúmenes que quedan unidos entre sí mediante originales cubiertas, las cuales se van adaptando a los diferentes módulos. A fin de poder conseguir este sobrio y a la vez original proyecto, el material utilizado fue principalmente el acero, cuya resistencia permite utilizar los techos para exponer los coches.

Cet édifice destiné à la vente d'automobiles a vu le choix du jeu avec divers volumes restant unis entre eux par des toitures originales, s'adaptant aux différents modules. Afin de matérialiser ce projet à la fois sobre et original, l'acier a été le matériau utilisé principalement. Sa résistance permet d'utiliser les toits pour exposer les voitures.

Per questo edificio destinato alla vendita di automobili, si è scelto di giocare con vari volumi connessi tra loro mediante originali coperture che si adattano pian piano ai diversi moduli. Per poter ottenere questo progetto sobrio e al contempo originale, il materiale utilizzato è stato principalmente l'acciaio, la cui resistenza permette di utilizzare i soffitti come vetrine per le auto.

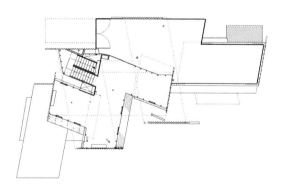

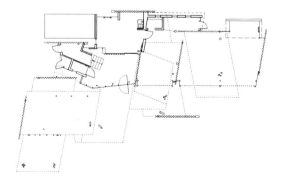

This steel building, whose function was to obtain drinking water, was erected in the middle of a public park. Its unusual appearance is a far cry from the purification plants built until now. These forms come from the desire to create an ecological building, in which everything is designed to take full advantage of renewable energy.

Inmitten eines öffentliche Parks steht dieses Stahlgebäude, das der Trinkwassergewinnung dient. Diese Kläranlage sieht ganz anders aus, als man es bisher gewohnt war. Die Formen entstanden, da man eine ökologisches Gebäude geschaffen hat, bei dem die rückgewinnbare Energie maximal genutzt wird.

Situado en medio de un parque público, este edificio de acero cumple la función de obtener agua potable. Su inusual aspecto está muy alejado del de las plantas de purificación construidas hasta ahora. Las formas de esta construcción tienen su origen en la voluntad de crear un edificio ecológico en el que todo está pensado para aprovechar al máximo las energías renovables.

Au cœur d'un parc public, cet édifice construit en acier a pour fonction d'assurer la génération d'eau potable. Son aspect inhabituel est passablement éloigné de celui des stations d'épuration construites jusqu'à présent. Ces formes trouvent leur origine dans la volonté de créer un bâtiment écologique où tout est pensé afin de tirer le meilleur parti des énergies renouvelables.

La funzione principale di questo edificio, in acciaio, eretto in mezzo a un parco pubblico, era di ottenere dell'acqua potabile. Il suo insolito aspetto si allontanava dagli impianti di purificazione costruiti finora. Le singolari forme rispondono alla volontà di creare un edificio ecologico in cui tutto è pensato per sfruttare al massimo le energie rinnovabili.

The architects designed this impressive tower, containing the most important books from the Medical University library, as an altar to wisdom. The structure, made from glass and steel, was positioned in the very center of the transept of an old church, a space full of symbolism and meaning.

Die Architekten entwarfen diesen beeindruckenden Turm, in dem die wichtigsten Bücher der Bibliothek der Medizinischen Fakultät gezeigt werden, so als ob es sich um einen Altar der Weisheit handeln würde. Die Struktur besteht aus Stahl und Glas und befindet sich in der Mitte der Vierung der alten Kirche, ein Raum voller Symbolik und Bedeutung.

Como si se tratara de un altar a la sabiduría, los arquitectos diseñaron esta impresionante torre en la que se muestran los libros más importantes que se conservan en la biblioteca de la universidad de medicina. La estructura, realizada con acero y cristal, se colocó en el centro mismo del crucero de una antigua iglesia, un espacio lleno de simbolismo y significado.

Comme si d'un autel au savoir il s'agissait, les architectes ont conçu cette tour impressionnante où exposer les livres les plus importants conservés dans la bibliothèque de la faculté de médecine. La structure, réalisée en acier et en verre, a été disposée au centre même de la croisée d'une ancienne église, un espace empli de symbolisme et de signifié.

Come se si trattasse di un altare alla saggezza, gli architetti hanno disegnato questa enorme torre dove mettere in mostra i volumi più importanti conservati nella biblioteca della facoltà di medicina. La struttura, realizzata in acciaio e vetro, è stata collocata proprio in mezzo alla crociera di un'antica chiesa, uno spazio carico di significato e simbolismo.

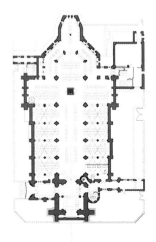

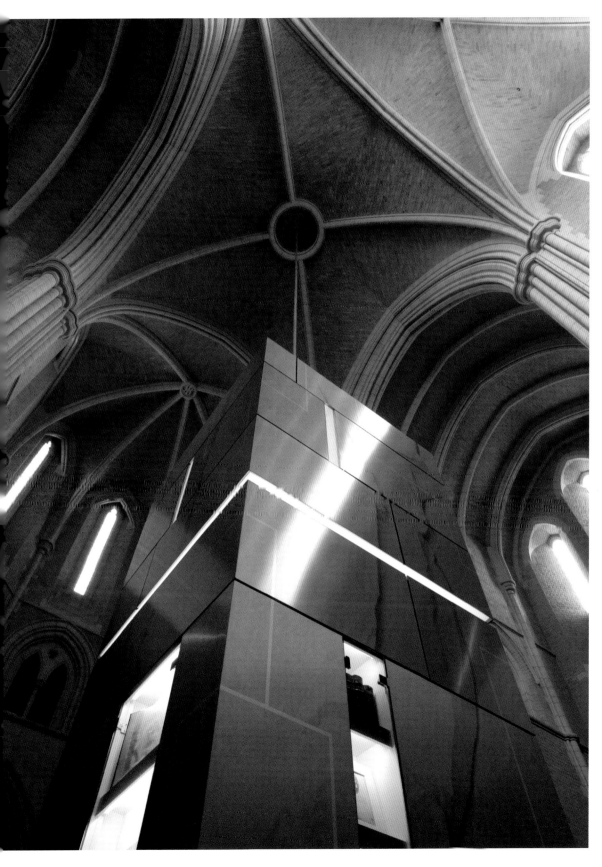

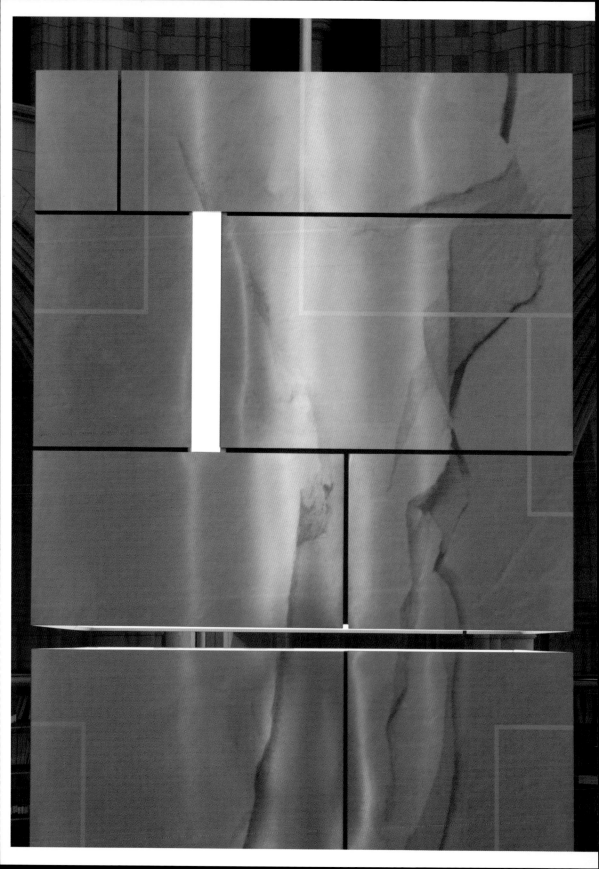

Despite the original commission being to create a venue on top of a car park, the result was this large public space, which could host a variety of activities, from exhibitions to markets. Galvanized steel was used to make the structures, sign boards, stairs and street furniture, mainly as a "deployé" mesh.

Im Laufe eines Projektes, bei dem zunächst nur ein Grundstück über einer Tiefgarage umgestaltet werden sollte, entstand dieser große öffentliche Raum, der für verschiedene Zwecke genutzt werden kann, z. B. Ausstellungen oder Märkte. Für die Strukturen, Trenn-und Hinweislemente, Treppen und Straßenmöbel wurde verzinkter Stahl verwendet, vor allem gewalzter Maschendraht.

A pesar de que el primer encargo era el de habilitar un solar para un *parking*, el resultado fue este gran espacio público en el que se pueden realizar diversas actividades, desde exposiciones hasta mercados. Para la realización de las estructuras, vallas, señalizaciones, escaleras y mobiliario urbano, se utilizó el acero galvanizado, principalmente a modo de malla "déployé".

Bien que la commande initiale ait porté sur la préparation d'un terrain sur un parking, c'est un vaste espace public qui est né, permettant d'accueillir une foule d'activités, depuis des marchés jusqu'à des expositions. L'acier galvanisé, principalement sous forme de maille déployée, a permis de réaliser les structures, clôtures, signalisations, escaliers et mobilier urbain.

Nonostante l'incarico originale fosse stato quello di riabilitare la superficie posta al di sopra di un parcheggio, il risultato finale è stato questo grande spazio pubblico dove poter realizzare diverse attività, da mostre a mercati. Per tutte le strutture, le recinzioni, la segnaletica, le scale e la mobilia urbana è stato utilizzato l'acciaio, principalmente a modo di rete stirata ("déployé").

Situated in the middle of a site with stables and polo pitches, this steel clad pavilion has been built over a bunker from 1936, that formed part of a defensive military line. The space, used for commercial purposes, comprises a single bedroom with a large window. The steel structure, with visible joins, has a mesh surface accentuating the construction's futuristic character.

Dieser mit Stahl verkleidete Pavillon liegt inmitten eines Grundstücks mit Ställen und Golfplatz und wurde im Jahr 1936 über einem Bunker errichtet, der zu einer militärischen Verteidigungslinie gehörte. Das zu kommerziellen Zwecken genutzte Gebäude besteht aus einem einzigen Raum mit einem großen Fenster. Die Oberfläche dieser Stahlstruktur mit unsichtbaren Fugen ist ein Flechtwerk, das den futuristischen Charakter des Gebäudes noch betont.

Ubicado en medio de un solar con establos y campos de polo, este pabellón revestido de acero ha sido construido sobre un búnker del año 1936, que formaba parte de una línea de defensa militar. El espacio, destinado a fines comerciales, consiste en una habitación única con una gran ventana. La estructura de acero, con juntas invisibles, cuenta en su superficie con un entramado que acentúa el carácter futurista de la construcción.

Situé au coeur d'un espace doté d'étables et d'un terrain de polo, ce pavillon habillé d'acier était construit sur un bunker datant de 1936, formant partie d'une ligne de défense militaire. L'espace à usage commercial est constitué d'une pièce unique avec une grande baie vitrée. La superficie de la structure d'acier, aux joints invisibles, est habillée d'un lattis qui accentue le caractère futuriste de la construction.

Situato in un terreno caratterizzato dalla presenza di varie stalle e campi da polo, questo padiglione rivestito d'acciaio è stato costruito su un bunker del 1936, che faceva parte di una linea di difesa militare. Lo spazio, destinato ad uso commerciale, consiste in un unico ambiente con una grande finestra. La struttura in acciaio, con giunti invisibili, mostra una trama superficiale che ne accentua il carattere futurista.

BCQ – Baena, Casamor & Quera Arquitectes
Sant Magí 11-13, 1.º
08006 Barcelona, Spain
P +34 932 372 721
mail@bcq.es
www.bcq.es
Port Forum 2004
© BCQ – Baena, Casamor & Quera Arquitectes

Bernard Tschumi Architects
227 West 17th Street
New York, NY 10011, United States
P + 1 212 807 6340
www.tschumi.com
Concert Hall and Exhibition Complex
© Esto Images / Peter Mauss, Christian Richters
Vacheron Constantin Headquarters and Watch Factory
© Esto Images / Peter Mauss, Christian Richters

Conix Architecten
Cockerilkaari 18
B-200 Antwerp, Belgium
P + 32 3 259 11 30
info@conixarchitecten.be
www.conixarchitecten.be
Atomium Renovation
© Atomiumvzw-SabamBelgium2006-Vitra,
Tom Vack, Serge Brison

Crepain Binst Architecture
Vlaanderenstraat 6
B2000 Antwerp, Belgium
P + 32 3 213 61 61
mail@crepainbinst.be
www.crepainbinst.be
Feyen House
© Ludo Noël
Gyke House
© Toon Grobet
Offices for Renson
© Coolens & Deleuil, Ludo Noël, Toon Grobet
Offices for Wauters
© Toon Grobet

David Jay Weiner
425 Park Avenue South
New York, NY 10016, United States
P + 1 212 696 4345
info@dweiner.com
www.dweiner.com
Zen Garden House
© David Jay Weiner

Delugan Meissl Associated Architects
Mittersteig 13 / 4
A-1040 Vienna, Austria
P +43 1 585 36 90
office@deluganmeissl.at
www.deluganmeissl.at
House Ray 1
© Rupert Steiner, Herta Hurnauss, Peter Rigaud

Frank Gehry & Partners
12541 Beatrice Street
Los Angeles, CA 90066, United States
P + 1 310 482 3000
info@foga.com
www.foga.com
Walt Disney Concert Hall
© Johannes Marburg

Gary Shoemaker Architects
80 Maiden Lane, # 1501
New York, NY 10038, United States
P + 1 212 766 9915
sungsoo@gsarchitects.com
www.gsarchitects.com
TSI, Transitional Services for New York
© Paul Warchol Photography

Giorgio Borruso Design
333 Washington Blvd
Marina del Rey, CA 90292, United States
P + 1 310 821 9224
Fila Store
© Benny Chan, Fotoworks
Miss Sixty Store
© Benny Chan, Fotoworks

Group A
Pelgrimstraat 3
3029 BH Rotterdam, The Netherlands
P + 31 10 244 01 93
info@groupa.nl
www.groupa.nl
Booster Station
© DigiDaan
Offices for Sabic
© Luuk Kramer

Holzer Kobler Architekturen
Ankerstrasse 3
CH-8004 Zürich, Switzerland
P + 41 1 240 52 00
mail@holzerkobler.ch
www.holzerkobler.ch
Biopolis
© Annette Fischer

J. J. Pan & Partners, Architects & Planners
21, Alley 12, Lane 118, Ren Ai Road, Section 3
Taipei, Taiwan 10657, Republic of China
P + 886 2 2701 2617
jjpp@jjpan.com
www.jjpan.com
Office, Horizon Design
© Jim Chang

Javier García Solera
Avenida Doctor Gadea 3, 3.º dcha.
03003 Alicante, Spain
P + 34 965 984 188
jgsdd@arquired.es
Noray Café
© David Frutos

John Friedman-Alice Kimm Architects
701 East 3rd Street, Suite 300
Los Angeles, CA 90013, United States
P + 1 213 253 4760
L.A. Designer Center
© Benny Chan, Fotoworks

Johnson Chou
56 Berkeley Street
Toronto, M5A 2W6 Ontario, Canada
P + 1 416 703 6777
mail@johnsonchou.com
www.johnsonchou.com
Womb. Work, Office, Mediation, Base
© Volker Sending Photography
Yolles Residence
© Volker Sending Photography

José María López & Manuel Ródenas
Isidoro de la Cierva 5, entlo.
30001 Murcia, Spain
P + 34 968 219 601
F + 34 968 220 871
estudio@rodenasarquitectos.com
Leisure Pavilion
© David Frutos

Jun Aoki
Harajuku New Royal Bldg. #701 3-38-11, Shibuya-ku
Tokyo 150-0001, Japan
www.aokijun.com
F + 81 3 3478 0508
White Chapel
© Daici Ano

Kazuhiko Oishi Architecture Atelier
7-2-7 Nishijin Sawara-ku
Fukuoka 814-000, Japan
P +81 92 823 0882
oishi.architect@jcom.home.ne.jp
Fabric Wall Residence
© Nacása & Partners

LAB Architecture Studio
Unit 300 Curtain House 134-146 Curtain Road
London EC2A 3AR, United Kingdom
P +44 20 7033 9193
info@labarchitecture.com
www.labarchitecture.com
Federation Square
© Trevor Mein, Peter Clarke, LAB Architecture Studio

M2-Nakatsuji Architect Atelier
1-3-5-601 Ebisu-Nishi, Shibuya-ku
Tokyo 150-0021, Japan
P +81 3 5459 0095
m-naka@mxj.mesh.ne.jp
www2u.biglobe.ne.jp / ~m-naka / e-index.html
F House
© Toshiharu Kitajima

MAP Arquitectos / Josep Lluís Mateo
Teodoro Roviralta 39
08022 Barcelona, Spain
P +34 932 186 358
www.mateo-maparchitect.com
CCIB Forum
© Infinite Light, AlbeFòrum Barcelona 2004 / Albert Masías

Massimiliano Fuksas
Piazza del Monte di Pietà 30
00186 Rome, Italy
P +39 06 6880 7871
office@fuksas.it
www.fuksas.it
New Milan Trade Fair
© Archivio Fuksas, Philippe Ruault

Olson Sundberg Kundig Allen Architects
159 South Jackson Street, Suite 600
Seattle, WA 98104, United States
P +1 206 624 5670
newinquiry@oskaarchitects.com
www.oskaarchitects.com
Chicken Point Cabin
© Undine Pröhl

On-A Lab
Doctor Rizal 8, local 1
08006 Barcelona, Spain
P +34 932 184 306
contact@on-a-lab.com
www.on-a-lab.com
5 Sentidos Lounge Bar
© On-A Lab

Ortiz León Arquitectos
Príncipe de Vergara 13
28001 Madrid, Spain
P +34 914 350 398
orlearq@ortizleon.com
www.ortizleon.com
Sanitas Offices in Madrid
© Jordi Miralles

RCR Arquitectes
Passeig de Blay 34, 2.º
17800 Girona, Spain
P +34 972 269 105
rcr@rcrarquitectes.es
www.rcrarquitectes.es
Bathing Pavilion
© Jordi Miralles

Renzo Piano Building Workshop
Via P. P. Rubens 29
16158 Genoa, Italy
P +39 0106 1711
italy@rpbw.com
www.rpbw.com
Paul Klee Zentrum
© Michel Denancé

Ron Arad Associates
62 Chalkfarm Road
NW1 8AN London, United Kingdom
P +44 20 7284 4963
info@ronarad.com
www.ronarad.com
Hotel Duomo
© Design Hotels

Santa-Rita Arquitectos / João Santa-Rita
R. Teixeira de Pascoais 21, 5ª
1700-364 Lisbon, Portugal
P +351 21 848 55 55
santaritaarq@sapo.pt
Restaurant in Oeiras
© FG+SG / Fernando Guerra

Shuhei Endo Architect Institute
6F, 3-21, Suehiro-cho, Kita-ku
Osaka 530-0053, Japan
P +81 6 6312 7455
endo@paramodern.com
www.paramodern.com
Rooftecture O-K
© Yoshiharu Matsumura
Rooftecture S
© Yoshiharu Matsumura
Springtecture OT
© Yoshiharu Matsumura

Steven Holl Architects
450 West 31st Street, 11th floor
New York, NY 10001, United States
P +1 212 629 7262
mail@stevenholl.com
www.stevenholl.com
Whitney Water Purification Facility and Park
© Paul Warchol, Andy Ryan, Steven Holl Architects

Surface Architects
51 Scrutton Street
London EC2A 4PJ, United Kingdom
P +44 20 7729 1030
sam@surfacearchitects.com
www.surfacearchitects.com
Queen Mary Medical School Library
© Killian O'Sullivan

Torres Nadal
González Adalid 6, 3.º C
30001 Murcia, Spain
P +34 968 214 685
estudio@torresnadal.com
www.torresnadal.com
Car Park in Murcia
© David Frutos

Un Studio
Stadhouderskade 113
PO Box 75381
1070 AJ Amsterdam, The Netherlands
P +31 20 570 20 40
info@unstudio.com
www.unstudio.com
Tea House
© Christian Richters

© 2007 daab
cologne london new york

published and distributed worldwide by
daab gmbh
friesenstr. 50
d - 50670 köln

p + 49 - 221 913 927 0
f + 49 - 221 - 913 927 20

mail@daab-online.com
www.daab-online.com

publisher ralf daab
rdaab@daab-online.com

creative director feyyaz
mail@feyyaz.com

editorial project by loft publications
© 2007 loft publications

editor and texts daniela santos quartino and isabel artigas

layout laura millán
english translation jay noden
german translation susanne engler
french translation michel ficerai
italian translation maurizio siliato

printed in china

isbn 978-3-937718-65-1